UPHELD *in the* BATTLE

Upheld in the Battle is an honestly portrayed revelation of how God moves, speaks, and gently guides us through the valleys and deserts of our lives. Linda Jo humbly weaves stories of personal pain with scripture, producing a beautiful portrait of lives touched by the hand of God just when all seems lost. *Upheld in the Battle* is well written and carefully crafted to create a pleasant blend of real life and tutorage.

—**Jan Cline**, author of *A Heart Out of Hiding*, founder and director of the Inland NW Christian Writers Conference

Upheld in the Battle is a timely must-read for the Body of Christ, especially those facing life's most difficult circumstances. Through this story, you will share in the fruit of transformation; and special God-anointed words will encourage, challenge, and inspire you in a personal way. Regardless of what you're walking through at this very moment, God will use it for your good and for His glory. He promised!

—**Therese Marszalek**, author, speaker, and founder of Therese Marszalek Ministries

Linda Jo Reed knows firsthand the challenges of walking a difficult and painful life path. But that's not the point of her book. In *Upheld in the Battle*, she shows why she can say with unflinching certainty that God is faithful. Even in the toughest times. And in her practical and relatable book, she shows why we can say it, too. Thank you, Linda Jo. I wish I'd had this book when I was stumbling down my own difficult road.

—**Kay Strom**, speaker and author of the *Grace In Africa* trilogy

UPHELD *in the* BATTLE

Living in Heroic Faith

LINDA JO REED

You are my servant, I have chosen
you and have not cast you away:
Fear not, for I am with you; Be not dismayed,
for I am your God.
I will strengthen you,
Yes, I will help you,
I will uphold you with My righteous right hand.
—Isaiah 41:9b–10

NEW YORK

UPHELD *in the* BATTLE
Living in Heroic Faith

ISBN 978-1-61448-652-7 paperback
ISBN 978-1-61448-653-4 eBook
Library of Congress Control Number: 2013933441

Morgan James Publishing
The Entrepreneurial Publisher
5 Penn Plaza, 23rd Floor
New York City, New York 10001
(212) 655-5470 office • (516) 908-4496 fax
www.MorganJamesPublishing.com

Cover Design by:
Rachel Lopez
www.r2cdesign.com

Interior Design by:
Bonnie Bushman
bonnie@caboodlegraphics.com

To daughter Angela and son Jeff
God kept them safe in faith.
and
To Nancy and Wayne Bentz
These dear friends kindly and patiently
walked me through discovery.
Thank you.

TABLE OF CONTENTS

FOREWORD

LINDA JO REED'S *Upheld in the Battle* is a timely must read for the Body of Christ, especially those facing life's most difficult circumstances. This anointed writer and gifted teacher of God's Word transparently shares her journey through the darkest season of her life where she was tested and tried in the blazing fires of trial. As you'll see, instead of trying to run from the flames of affliction, Linda Jo chose to submit herself to God and endure His purifying process of transformation and growth. Because she embraced and walked with her Savior in the fire, she emerged in victory and now can help others find victory. You won't find a hint of smoke from the fires Linda Jo walked through; but instead, a fragrance of Jesus that is bringing hope to others facing seasons in the furnace of affliction.

I praise the Lord for Linda Jo's willingness to share her story, which again shows that, whatever the enemy intends for evil, God will use for the good of those who love Him. As a furnace survivor myself, I join Linda Jo to assure you that regardless of what you're walking through at this very moment, God will use it for your good and for His glory. He promised!

As you read the coming pages, you will partake of the fruit of the transformation God did throughout Linda Jo's journey. You'll also find nuggets of special blessings as she shares intimate words that God spoke to her along the journey. I believe those words, anointed by God, will encourage, challenge, and inspire to you in a personal way, as they did me.

Upheld in the Battle demonstrates one of my favorite scriptures from 2 Corinthians 1:3, 4: "Blessed be the God and Father of our Lord Jesus Christ, the Father of mercies and God of all comfort, who comforts us in all our tribulation, that we may be able to comfort those who are in any trouble, with the comfort with which we ourselves are comforted by God." May you receive comfort that will inspire you to live in heroic faith from the comfort Linda Jo received from the God and Father of our Lord Jesus Christ.

Blessings in Christ,
Therese Marszalek
Author, speaker, and founder of
Therese Marszalek Ministries
www.theresemarszalek.com

ACKNOWLEDGMENTS

MY WRITERS GROUP CO-LEADER always says it is a group project to produce a good piece of writing. She is right. It is also good practice and good manners to thank those in your group. I would like to do that here.

My children, Angela and Jeff, lived in this story and then let me write about them.

My husband's family and my family also lived in this story and have graciously supported me in writing it. Thank you, dear ones.

My friends Connie, Carolyn, and Arlie let me use their stories. Also, my prayer group at my day job read, reread, and edited. I want to thank other friends who had a part as well.

My Tea Counsel group cried with me through the situations as they happened, then encouraged me to write the book.

The Scribettes, my writers group, taught me how to make words work and encouraged me along the way.

My lovely Llamas group encouraged me to keep taking the steps.

My friend Laurie gave me invaluable suggestions that improved my manuscript immensely. My friends Therese and Jan taught and encouraged me, and Anita saved my sanity during the editing process.

Pastor Steve Flora was kind to let me take, use, and exploit his sermon any way I wanted to do so.

My friends Nancy and Wayne gave their love and empathy to help me understand years of confusion—this was a God-changing life experience for me.

Finally, the staff at Morgan James Publishing guided me through the stages of production with patience and kindness.

PROLOGUE

DRIVING HOME ALL I COULD think of was putting up my aching feet. Numerous customers kept me running all day, and resting in my comfortable chair with my feet propped up topped my list for the evening.

I opened the door to hear my frantic children crying, "Wake up, Daddy! We can't wake Daddy up!"

Instantly I scanned the scene. The TV blared from the corner and the light above spotlighted the back of my husband's head as one child pulled on his arm and another child shook his shoulder, only to have him settle back into the easy chair. How long had this been going on? He was supposed to be caring for them while I went to work.

Dean had passed out in this chair many times before, but not when he would put our young children in danger. My muscles tensed and my jaw tightened. In seconds, I prioritized my responsibilities. My children needed attention. Number one was to make things as normal for them as possible.

"Ok, kids, let Daddy sleep. It's time for you to get ready for bed. You know what to do—baths are first, let's go." I shepherded them down the hall, a child close under each arm.

After the baths, we read Bible stories together on a child's bed, as we did every night. This time we read Psalm 23.

"'The Lord is my Shepherd.' Do you know that this means God will always take care of us, no matter what?" I saw wide-eyed nods and continued to read. "'I shall not want. He makes me to lie down in green pastures. He leads me by still waters…'"

The children took their turns reading, too. In this way I could monitor their reading skills as well as teach them about God. Tonight, they needed the reassurance this calming psalm could give them.

"Daddy will be fine. You'll see in the morning." We prayed and I tucked them into bed. Security was restored and they went to sleep.

Now I had to rouse Dean and get him to bed. As I stalked up to the chair, anger changed to fear. I stared. No movement. No chest rising and falling. I reached for his wrist searching for a pulse. Nothing. I laid my ear to his chest. No heartbeat. In panic, I touched the skin of his forearm. His warm skin reassured me. I pulled up an eyelid. A dilated, staring pupil met my shocked gaze.

CHAPTER ONE

A LIVING SACRIFICE

Learning to Let Go of Earthly Hopes and Crushed Dreams

I beseech you therefore, brethren, by the mercies of God, that you present your bodies a living sacrifice, holy, acceptable to God, which is your reasonable service. And do not be conformed to this world, but be transformed by the renewing of your mind, that you may prove what is that good and acceptable and perfect will of God. (Rom. 12:1–2)

L ight flashed and the man was propelled off his horse and on his hands and knees before a frightening Presence.

"Saul, Saul, why are you persecuting me?"

Awful dread must have crept over Saul as he asked, "Who are you, Lord?"

Then came the answer he probably suspected he would hear, "I am Jesus, whom you are persecuting …"

In trembling astonishment, he asked, "What do you want me to do?" And the Lord said to him, "Arise and go into the city and you will be told what you must do." Saul arose from the ground, a blind man, who had to be led.[1]

In an instant, his dreams were smashed, his identity was taken, and all his preparations and plans for the life he thought that he would live were wasted. Instead of being the man in command of his destiny and that of others, now, as a blind man, he needed others to lead him around and had to wait for further instructions.

Raised as a Jewish aristocrat with social position, a stellar education, Roman citizenship (which would open all doors to him), and perfect credentials, Saul was a Man With A Future. That is, until a lightning bolt shot him out of the saddle, killed his earthly dreams, and blinded his earthly eyes so he could see the Truth.

I never anticipated a bolt of lightning waiting for me either when I dreamed my dreams and made plans for my future.

Everyone loves a wedding. The relatives and friends come together, all dressed up and wearing their best smiles, to help the bride and groom celebrate the beginning of a new life together.

Humorous stories are often shared about wedding jitters. I have a memory of sunshine through stained glass highlighting the shaking hem of my bridegroom's tuxedo as I walked up the aisle on my father's arm. After the part in the ceremony that transferred my future from father to husband, I found myself holding up that nervous bridegroom. We laughed about it afterwards, but it seemed to me later that it was an indicator of what would come.

As pink roses on a cake, fancy dresses, veil, and a sporty jaguar faded away to memory, everyday life stepped in. Perhaps it is true with nearly every newlywed couple that high expectations must meet with down-to-earth reality. I discovered my husband could not meet all my needs. Nor could I fulfill his desires as he wished. Serious issues surfaced and I began seeking God for solace.

After my conversion to Christ, my constant prayer was, "Please, God, let my life be a living sacrifice, holy and acceptable to you." Serving this God I had just met was a priority. As the Romans 12 scripture said, I wanted my mind transformed, and I wanted to know what it meant to prove the will of God.[2]

It's funny how God takes us at our word.

As a young wife and mother, if anyone had asked me what a "living sacrifice" might look like, I am sure I would have said, "Huh?" With my life in front of me, I was ready for a great adventure, but I was unprepared for what that adventure would involve.

We had two children, a girl and a boy, and I expected to live what I considered a normal family life. However, life has a way of surprising us and my illusions were soon shattered.

My husband, Dean, was involved in an accident at work that caused a back injury. It was the beginning of a landslide of back injuries. His father passed away about the same time and this left him unable to cope. Over the years, his physical health deteriorated with more surgeries and other issues. He developed drug and alcohol addictions, and it became apparent that there were some mental disorders as well.

When I asked God to make a living sacrifice of my life, I wanted to honor God. I certainly did *not* mean traveling this road of suffering. Who of us does? Often I cried out, "God! Fix it! Hurry!"

Cutting across everything I ever believed or wanted was the idea that God might ask me to give up my desires and hopes in the day-to-day experiences of my life. In the Scripture, God called this my reasonable service, but I thought He couldn't possibly mean it. Sacrificing everything clashes with our own plans, and we don't want to go there. However, some of us find that we are in that place and not by choice.

For me, sacrificing meant letting go of my dream of the perfect marriage. I thought marriage meant I would have a wonderful companion who understood me and shared every dream. My husband would go to work to support us. I would stay home with the kids. We would go on wonderful vacations, and I would get to pursue my hobbies.

Instead, I learned to let go of expectations and even of who I hoped to become one day. In embracing a caretaker role that took a lifetime to unfold in a variety of ways, I allowed God to fashion me His way in order to serve Him best where He placed me. I learned that God had other plans for me than those I had for myself.

God calls this letting go "holy and acceptable." So what do we do if we are called to sacrifice?

Acknowledge Who Is In Charge

As my vain attempts to manage and control our lives constantly failed, I gained some familiarity with surrender. I didn't like it. I watched my hopes and dreams slipping away, and I could do nothing to hang onto them. I begged for miracles.

One evening, while writing desperate prayers in my journal, I heard God's words in my head. I asked Him to help me follow Him and to study His Word, the Bible, and to live it one day at a time. I could go no further.

Take your life off hold, Daughter. Stop looking for the time when circumstances will change to what you want. You are putting that first in your life, and not Me.

"I am? What do you mean, Lord?"

I have said I will give you the desires of your heart according to My will. Put Me first. Seek Me daily. Talk to Me. I want your companionship, not just a few words here and there. Talk to Me. Ask Me anything. Daily.

If I continued to insist on living and clinging to the tatters of my earthly hopes and dreams, then I was blind to the greatness that God wanted to call forth in me.

"Lord," I wrote, "How do I get joy in my heart? It's so heavy."

I Am the Answer, the Truth, the Life, and the Way. Joy begins when you seek Me with all your heart. I want your love as a lover who can't stand to be parted from the beloved. Will you accept Me on those terms?

I caught my breath.

"Is that ok?" I wondered, "or is it irreverent?" God yearned for me to desire Him. Like *that*? In the midst of the whirlwinds of life, God really comes!

It's true that we can't honestly live until we are ready to die. Only then can we live generously, prepared to give all we are and all we have to the One who loves us with all His being. And only then are we ready to give up our plans for something "greater."

Even as God loves us, He expects us to relinquish our lives to Him. This furthers His eternal kingdom. It may not look very pleasant to us, but He has the plan. It may include very difficult situations. It may include major health issues.

My good friend, Connie, discovered this one morning when she woke up and readied herself for work. She got in her car and drove to her job just as she did every day. However, twenty minutes after sitting down at her desk, Connie slumped over unconscious. She was suffering a major stroke. Her boss, a doctor, found her quickly, and in a short time she was hospitalized. For several days her family and friends held their breath not knowing if she would live or die. She was not in charge. What made this situation unusual is that Connie was a young and beautiful woman on the threshold of a new life as her children were just leaving home to attend college. Who would have guessed that such a thing would happen?

Connie survived her stroke, but it changed her life forever. Her steps were literally ordered by others for some time. Through a lengthy therapy, she recovered well, but now she lives a very different life than what she had planned.

She says, "If you truly live life, it is *always* risky. That's what I had to give up: the notion that life, if you lived it right, would be safe. But not even God is safe." For her, the acknowledgment that God is in charge was embodied in C.S. Lewis' famous line in *The Lion, The Witch and the Wardrobe* when Mr. Beaver described Aslan: "Who said anything about safe? 'Course he isn't safe. But he's good."[3]

The notion that God should be safe is not particularly biblical when we consider that by safe we mean that God should do the things we want Him to do so we can be comfortable. Instead, God may do things that look like disaster in our eyes. However, God will always do what is best in His great plan.

God is in charge. God is good. Are we paying attention?

Be Not Conformed To This World

The challenge of living a life counter to what was safe and normal brought on much emotional and spiritual pain. I could choose to conform to the world's idea of safe and normal. I would then have society's permission to run from my situation. That would be much easier and definitely more comfortable.

On the other hand, I felt the tug of a higher calling to stay and see the situation through. Yet, even before I could determine the choice, I had to answer the fundamental question of whether something unknown could be more important than my earthly happiness and comfort level.

"God! Why does it have to be so *hard*? Why don't you just *fix* it?"

One summer when my children were elementary school age, we went on a road trip vacation. I did most of the driving. The kids stared out the back seat windows and my husband snored away in the passenger seat.

Quiet reigned momentarily, but not in my soul. I wrestled with my choices and with feeling abandoned by God.

Unexpectedly, I heard, "Trust in the Lord and wait patiently for Him."

I started in my seat and gripped the steering wheel.

"Trust in the Lord and wait patiently for Him."

I glanced at my daughter through the rear view mirror. She was still gazing out the window.

"Trust in the Lord and wait patiently for Him." That sweet child's voice repeated the phrase for the third time. She thought she was memorizing Scripture, but it shot like a bolt to my heart. Through her, God reminded me that He had not left me and expected me to follow those instructions.

With His reassurance to continue on this spiritual road, I later read His encouragement, substituting "he" for "I" or "me," through Psalm 37:24, "Though he fall, he shall not be utterly cast down; for the Lord upholds him with His hand."

A quiet voice within reminded me that God was still my loving Father, who would gently guide me as I followed Him. He would take me where I thought I could not go. As a father takes his precious child by the hand and walks through a difficult pathway, the child slips, but the firm grip of his father holds him upright. So God walked with me.

I chose to stay in my marriage. I came to the conclusion that if I ran from this painful plan, I would miss the fruit it would yield in time. To help me cope, God brought me wonderful counselors, help through group sessions with others in similar situations, a loving family, and a cheerful community of believers to love and support me. I found that living sacrifice happens in layers. It's not something that can be learned and it's done. It's *living*, after all, and therefore, ongoing.

So then, to "be not conformed to this world" must mean more than just the crushing of dreams. If we want more than what this world has to offer, the mystery is that it comes through the living sacrifice. As we go through this fire, we will reap the rewards on the other side.

God may appear to be an enigma to us, but He wants to be known. He asks us to trust Him. He asks us to train our minds through reading Scriptures, praying, and seeking wise counsel; to look to Him when the going gets tough. He will equip us to make choices and do things that seem far beyond us as we go through the trials that change our thinking processes. In this way, we learn of adventures in the spirit. We learn to live according to the deep places in our souls instead of on the surface of life where mere happenstance happiness is not enough.

Only He sees our secret torments and hears the cries that reverberate through our souls. He is the only one who can speak to those secret places with His soothing love and care. God's ear is *always* open to us. His answers are constant when we call, though we may not recognize them or like them. He doesn't require special sacrifices to attract His attention, He just wants our hearts. But this doesn't mean He never asks for sacrifices. Sometimes that is the only way to build character in us, or pry our fingers off something we think we want, or move us through a situation.

Our sacrifices will never be a criterion to get God's attention or a means by which we can move Him to act for us. He is aware of our manipulations.

God calls us to renew our minds. So that we may do so, He gives us His Word, the Bible, as the place to go for our help. As we read it, truth seeps into our souls with cool refreshment. Our circumstances may not change, but through the words we read, and through our prayers, comes a sense of comfort, something beyond ourselves.

Victor Hugo is reputed to have said, "There are thoughts which are prayers. There are moments when, whatever the posture of the body, the soul is on its knees."[4] I don't understand how my soul can be on its knees when I am otherwise busy, but I know that somehow God hears my deepest prayers even when I haven't uttered a word.

In those things that cannot be seen, somehow, as we come to Him in surrender, He transforms our souls. As hope renews our minds, we can go forward in the circumstances of our lives knowing we are not alone.

Our Dreams, God's Dreams

When I came to a place where I realized my dreams were gone, the agony went beyond feeling. My bewildered soul screamed the questions within.

"How could life betray me like this?"

"Where do I go from here?"

"How do I fill the black hole inside?"

"What do I do with the grief and the anger? Or the blame?"

"Can God be trusted?"

The American Dream was never God's goal for us. Knowing Him, His glory, and becoming like Him is at the forefront of the plans God has for us. This is our great discovery when we give up our hopes and dreams to allow Him to create a new life for us. Yet, it's such a struggle to accept His claim on our lives.

He shows us the promise of great adventures ahead when we are willing to move out into the unknown with Him. It's much better than the American Dream!

As we live our lives on earth, we have no idea how big God's heart is toward us. We don't know how much He wants for us, nor how great are the plans He has for us. We don't understand how carefully He is crafting our lives.

He plants seeds of greatness into our souls. The dreams that God grows in us are what draw us to that greatness if we do not lose heart. Max Lucado said, "God always rejoices when we dare to dream. In fact, we are much like God when we dream. The Master exults in newness. He delights in stretching the old. He wrote the book on making the impossible possible."[5]

It isn't until we are ready to let go of our own crushed hopes and dreams that we are ready for the depths of knowing God. This is the place where only He can come into those deep chasms in our hearts that we are not aware of, touch us as He did Jacob when they wrestled at the foot of the ladder, and Jacob demanded God's blessing (Gen. 32:24–31). Only in those deep agonies does He burn his Spirit into us in such a way that we are branded by Him forever.

"The eyes of your understanding being enlightened; that you may know what is the hope of His calling, what are the riches of the glory of His inheritance in the saints," (Eph. 1:18). In reference to this scripture, B. J. Hoff says:

> Too many times, Lord, when I see a dream die,
> I lose hope because my plans have come to nothing.
> Help me to remember that your love is always greater
> than my disappointments ... and your plan for my life
> is always better than my brightest dreams.[6]

What does it take to live in heroic faith? Over time, I learned that we bow before God in dependence on His power to lift us, preserve us, go before us, defend us, guard us, and teach us. By necessity, and through prayer, Bible study, and listening to teaching, I brought all aspects of my life to Him so that He could fit me into His kingdom in the place where I would be most effective on this earth. Continually I wondered if I would be willing to take the risks to fit that place. Would I be willing to trust Him to make new dreams an actuality in my life?

Waking Up and Growing Up

We are trying to make the best of this fallen world in which we live. We long to have our spiritual eyes open so we can see what is beyond the suffering we are experiencing. We want to understand what God has for us if we can only endure. We want to know if God really *will* be our strength, yet if we do not press forward, we will not discover this truth. Only in the determined action of pressing forward and proving Him will we find out what is the good, and perfect, and acceptable will of God.

What is our reasonable service? We consider that our service is through the Cross of Christ. We consider that Christ yearns for an intimate relationship with us. Why would He go through the torture of crucifixion if not because His heart bursts with longing for us? Perhaps reasonable service means looking away from all we have known before in order to join in loving friendship with this One who gave up everything because of His great love for us.

Then, conceivably, reasonable service extends to serving others without visible return. If we serve only to expect something to come back to us, then it really is no service at all. Jesus came to earth as a man. He went to the Cross as a lamb. He did it alone to all human perceptions. He did not expect return or recompense. He left it all in the hands of His Father.

Service without expectation. Service without return. What a radical concept.

This way of sacrifice and service is hard, no doubt about it. Sometimes we travel this road kicking and screaming. However, it is worth the price. The rewards come from God Himself.

"Well done, good and faithful servant" (Matt. 25:21).

Go into the land and enjoy what I have prepared for you. We persevere. God is pleased.

Sufficient Grace

Next to worshipping God, I think pleasing Him is the highest goal. In this chaotic world, as we intend to please Him, we have purpose.

As we acknowledge that He is in charge of our lives and we are not, we open ourselves to His leading.

We learn to make choices for health, even to seeking help when pressures push us too hard.

We make decisions about what we will allow our minds to dwell on.

We think about how God may replace our visions and goals with His and we determine to follow His best plan.

We regard what may be our reasonable service and act upon it; then we discover that His grace is always enough.

"I see no reason for my suffering," I said one day to God. "I can't see where it's suffering for you at all. It's plain, senseless suffering."

God showed me how Paul, in the book of Acts, suffered a great many things. He was stoned, shipwrecked, bitten by a snake, and suffered physical ailments.

"Yeah, but Paul was obviously suffering for you," I protested. "He was jailed for preaching–shipwrecked because Satan didn't want him getting to Rome and showing the world who Jesus was and making disciples. It's obvious. He was called; he was an apostle."

So, do you think I can't call people now? God responded. *You are seeing Paul's life from an historical point of view. The tapestry is already woven in the Scripture. You can see the whole scope of Paul's sufferings. His earthly life is over and recorded. You see it all at a glance. Do you suppose Paul always knew what was going on each time something happened to him? Don't you suppose there were times when Paul said, 'I see no point to this?*

I started thinking. I suppose maybe Paul could have wondered. He could only see the moment, just as I can only see the moment. Maybe it's possible that someday someone could look at my life and say, "Yeah, sure, but it was obvious that *she* was suffering for the Lord."

God told Paul, "My grace is sufficient for you" (2 Cor. 12:9).

He tells us the same thing and we can believe Him.

CHAPTER TWO

A COMMANDMENT

Obeying Through Abiding

Abide in Me, and I in you. As the branch cannot bear fruit of itself, unless it abides in the vine, neither can you, unless you abide in Me. (John 15:4)

By this My Father is glorified, that you bear much fruit; so you will be My disciples. (John 15:8)

Abiding in Heaven's Heart
When my daughter, Angela, was four years old, she asked if Jesus is Heaven's Heart. I said, "Yes."

And … *we* are the love of His heart. God's theme has always been the same towards us.

I want you with me!

Doesn't this grab you?

The whole Bible is about God's love affair with His people on earth. Beginning with the beginning, in a garden, when God walked in the cool of the evening with Adam and Eve; to Moses, where God's people stood between the sea and a vengeful king, and God told them to stand still and see what He would do for them. And the Gospel of John, where Jesus says, "As the Father loved Me, I also have loved you; abide in My love" (John 15:9).

Once we let the love of God grab our hearts, we begin to learn to abide, or live in His love. He tells us in John 15 that He will work in our affairs to show us how to live and that without Him; we can do nothing that will have any lasting value. He will cut away at all things that are worthless in our lives, even when it hurts, because we disagree with Him. He tells us that as we trust Him and let Him change us, our desires will become the kind of desires that He can delight to grant us when we ask.

Later in the chapter, it says that God *chooses* us! He chooses us for special projects that will have lasting value. "You did not choose Me, but I chose you and appointed you that you should go and bear fruit, and that your fruit should remain, that whatever you ask the Father in My Name, He may give you" (John 15:16).

What an awesome statement! He chooses us. He appoints us. He gives us special work to do. Our work will be lasting. In doing this work, we can ask Him anything and He will do it for us.

As we obey Him, we find great joy in pleasing Him and seeing what He will do in our lives.

I woke up one night from a dream that left me shaken. In the dream, bombs dropped from the sky like fireballs all around the neighborhood. In horror I watched as my husband ran down the street trying to dodge bombs. I braced myself on the front porch of my house under the protection of the roof and clutched my children close to me.

I awoke afraid and drenched in sweat.

I didn't expect to go back to sleep but I did very quickly, only to dream again.

This time I was the new owner of a house badly in need of repair. In spite of the ramshackle condition, I was pleased the house belonged to me. I awoke this time relaxed and with a sense of well-being.

I puzzled over those dreams. Although I knew nothing about dream interpretation, I knew these were significant. Most of my life I had dismissed dreams, but these did not go away. Several years later, the meanings became plain to me.

The situation at home constantly increased with tension. Strange, new difficulties arose all the time, and I had no idea how to respond. God is gracious to give us subtle warnings of things to come when we are alert to His voice speaking to us through the Holy Spirit.

In the first dream I believe God warned me that in the terrible times to come, Dean would try to escape but would be a moving target in the very act of escape. He would be hit over and over. As long as I abided under the cover of the porch and held my children close, we would be safe though the bombs would drop all around us.

This surely pictured the way our life together unfolded. With each situation, Dean sought ways of numbing pain, but only succeeded in increasing it. The children and I met with similar pain and we chose a different route. In spite of frequent panic, we prayed and waited for God's presence to comfort us. We read the Bible for instruction and looked for outside help wherever we could find it. We chose to abide in the place of safety.

The second dream referred to a house that represented the soul of a Christian, brand new, yet in dilapidated condition. The renovation would take time but it would be shaped eventually. Jesus moved into this house, and I could abide here safely with Him.

God had chosen and appointed me to do a specific work. It still lay ahead of me at that time, but the groundwork of that appointment was set in place.

God Who Sees

Her labored breathing nearly choked her as she fled from camp. How could her mistress be so cruel? She couldn't take it anymore.

How could God forget her like this? Had she not been an obedient servant to both her master and her mistress? How was it her fault that she carried her master's child when her mistress was unable to do so? She hadn't chosen this! It was thrust upon her. They planned this, and then blamed her because it was so.

The desert was hot—so hot! Where *was* that spring? Her tongue swelled with the longing for water. Gritty sand clung to her feet as the sandals slapped them and her robe stuck to her uncomfortably. Her neck steamed under her wet hair. She wiped a hand across it.

Why had she not planned her escape? She'd run out of crazed fear and anger.

"God! Protect my babe! Where *are* you?"

Suddenly the spring and small scrub trees appeared in front of her. She fell to her knees and with both hands scooped water all over herself in her desperation to drink.

Finally satisfied, she sat back, quietly taking stock of her situation. Alone–in the desert–with no food or provisions and pregnant. How could she be so stupid? Where was God?

"Hagar, Sarai's maid, where have you come from and where are you going?"

Hagar started and looked around. "I am fleeing the presence of my mistress," she admitted, knowing full well who called her.

"Return to your mistress and submit yourself under her hand."

God continued to talk to Hagar that day. He told her about the son she carried in her womb and that she would have a multitude of descendents. He assured her that He had heard her affliction.

God gave Hagar a vision far greater than the circumstances under which she suffered.

She called that place, "Beer Lahai Roi." It means, "Well of the One who lives and sees me."[1]

In spite of all the commotion and controversy that surrounded Hagar, it seems she felt invisible. She wondered if God saw her. Did anybody really *see* her or was she just a necessary component to making someone else's life work?

Hagar went back to the mistreatment of her mistress because she had encountered God's love for her. He gave her a future then told her to go and serve. She trusted in His love and intervention in her life to care for her and her child as she served a spiteful mistress. She chose to abide in God's love.

I can understand Hagar's feelings of invisibility and the desperation that sent her fleeing. My scrub tree was often my car on a hill at night where the stars in the dark sky represented God's face to me.

This is where I cried out, "where are you, God? Don't you see what's happening here? Do you see me at all?"

Oswald Chambers has proven to be a great friend to me through his insights in *My Utmost for His Highest*. He wrote that "song birds are taught to sing in the dark, and we are put into the shadow of God's hand until we learn to hear Him."[2]

After a storm of anguish passed while I sat in my dark car, I watched the stars shimmer. If there were no darkness, those beautiful lights could not be seen. The hand of God put them there. I gazed for a long time in the quiet as my soul was stilled.

So, was this the shadow of God's hand?

I began to understand that my God lives and reigns and all my enemies really are under His feet. He is the victor, no matter what I experience right now. He is still the Vine and I am a branch and my life comes from Him.

He assured me He saw my struggles and heard my cries. He saw the suffering, the sacrifice, and there would be more in years to come, but I should not be afraid.

Something sweet happens in an intimate darkness with God. We can sit quietly and listen for His voice. When it comes, it fills the soul with peace and we learn to be steadfast whatever course of events rules our lives.

Abide with Me. Walk with Me in purity of spirit and willingness of heart and I will take you far. The waters are deep, but the treasures are there. I will be with you. Walk this path I have set before you. Don't veer to the right or the left. I am with you. I am your loving Father.

After the struggle, I knew He saw me. He had a plan, a greater purpose for me even though I could not understand it then. He sent me back into the fray just as He did with Hagar. My obedience was to trust His love and intervention for me and my children just like Hagar. I, too, was learning how to abide in God's love.

A caretaker often blends into the background, not seen or heard, just a necessary component to making someone else's life work.

But, God sees. He *always* sees His beloved. Especially in the darkness.

Fruit In Abiding

As we continue to wait for God and obey Him, we find great joy in pleasing Him and seeing what He will do in our lives. Jesus told us the fruit of our obedience would be lasting.

Imagine a hot summer day and biting into a juicy, luscious peach. The sweetness permeates your mouth as your eyes close in ecstasy, and juice trickles down your chin and hands. Oh, what a heavenly blessing that is!

What did we do to deserve that wonderful peach? Nothing. It was a gift. It was chosen for us to enjoy. It was given in pleasure, for pleasure. What were we required to do to merit that peach? All we needed to do was to accept the gift and share the delight in it. Sometimes that is what bearing fruit in obedience means. It is a simple trust that the giver will give good things and we are to share them. We can believe it. Jesus said that we are His disciples as we bear fruit, and His Father is glorified.

What a different picture from the constant striving to do right. We must achieve. We must do. We must have something to show for our efforts or we think that God cannot see the work we have done and we are invisible.

God wants us to succeed. Just as we are cheerleaders for our own children, our Father in heaven is our chief cheerleader. His heart is constantly reaching out for us. Our obedience is more than just a doing of things.

Isaiah 32:15–20 gives an illustration of the blessings that the Spirit of God pours out upon the children of obedience. A progression begins in a desert. God pours His Spirit out and the desert becomes a fertile field, then a forest, where the righteous can dwell. The fruit of living rightly is peace and the effect of that is quietness and confidence forever. Blessing follows.

The wilderness of our hearts becomes a fruitful field, even a forest. As we learn of God and what He expects of us, our love for Him increases and spreads to those around us. As we keep our consciences clean before God, the effect of this, even in the midst of trying circumstances, is peace of mind. Through that peace comes quietness and trust because God dwells with us as we look to Him. *Forever.*

He says, "My people will dwell in a peaceful habitation, in secure dwellings, and in quiet resting places, though hail comes down on the forest and the city is brought low in humiliation. Blessed are you ..." (Isaiah 32:18).

Do you see the assurances? Even if hail comes down and we are leveled with the problems we face, we can still have peace of mind and trust that He will be with us to work for us. This is blessing indeed.

Garden Love

Obedience is in loving and longing to please the beloved. "Not My will, but Thine." This was the cry of Jesus in the garden after terrible agonies and wrestling; agonies and wrestling that we cannot possibly understand as worlds clashed and Jesus wept and sweat blood.

Abba! Daddy!

How His Father's heart must have wrenched when He heard that cry and could not save His beloved Son from what was coming.

Out of love–Father and Son–*gave each other up!*

Out of love for us, the ones they created together.

Jesus was obedient–*out of love*–and in the greater purpose, He opened up eternity for us!

Imagine!

When this began to glimmer in my mind, I knew that my choice would be to obey my Heavenly Father's will *out of love* for the One who suffered most for me.

My obedience would not be perfect or even pretty at times, but only possible through His grace. Maybe the far reaching effect in my life would go beyond this world and into eternity as well.

Faith Walking

As experience taught me more about abiding in God's love and then making decisions to obey Him, I learned that it must come by faith.

Through faith I could trust that God would come through for me even if I didn't have the right emotions in place. The Bible says that without faith, it is impossible to please God. We have seen that He is in love with us. He is *for* us. He wants us to succeed in this faith walk because He wants us to have His very best. We are His children.

Our obedience is to make that decision to exercise faith and trust that He will do what He says He will do for us.

This does not always make good common sense. Sometimes it goes directly against it. Oswald Chambers talks about trusting God in spite of our common sense. He asks, "Can you trust Jesus Christ where your common sense cannot trust Him?"[3] Wow! Do you want to look like a fool to your family and friends? I don't.

I ask myself if I can walk in faith and trust God when it looks ridiculous and the circumstances look like a lie.

The observation I looked for again came from Chambers, "Faith is unutterable trust in God; trust which never dreams that He will not stand by us ... what is your faith up against now? The test will prove your faith or kill it ... the final thing is confidence in Jesus."[4]

I look at my life and think, "This is crazy! None of it makes any sense."

Is this a faith walk? Every step.

Will Jesus go with me? Every step.

Will it all happen as He wills? Yes. I have no idea when or how or what that means, but the answer is still yes.

Am I crazy? By the world's standards, yes. However, I choose by obedience to walk by faith. What will God do?

"But may the God of all grace, who called us to His eternal glory by Christ Jesus, after you have suffered a while, perfect, establish, strengthen, and settle you" (1 Peter 5:10).

My faith is up against it totally. Is there any other way to live? No. There is no adventure greater than what God will take me through.

And, after obedience, what could be better than to have the hands of God personally perfect me, establish me, strengthen me, and settle me!

That is what God will do.

Chapter Three

Through Fire and Water

Learning About God's Protection

Fear not, for I have redeemed you; I have called you by your name; you are Mine. When you pass through the waters, I will be with you; And through the rivers, they shall not overflow you. When you walk through the fire, you shall not be burned, nor shall the flame scorch you. For I am the Lord your God, the Holy One of Israel, your Savior. (Isa. 43:1b–3a)

Check the Fruit

Mick was an elder in the Fellowship. He died on his 40th birthday in the summer. It marked the beginning of the end of a season for me.

The Fellowship began meeting three years earlier in response to a message on repentance. We left an established church because we wanted more than a Sunday club. We wanted to know God more deeply and be more responsive to whatever He may ask of us. Our leaders, who we called elders, were untrained young men that we thought had God's anointing to lead. At first much excitement drew us together on Sundays and other days as we sought to worship God and serve one another. We started gathering in homes then moved to a commercial site for a while.

Yet like the frog that sits in lukewarm water and doesn't notice when the heat turns up and cooks him, we, too, did not feel the heat.

As teachings grew more specific, I began to squirm in my seat at meetings. I questioned what I was hearing, but kept the doubts silent because the peer pressure would be too great.

Our elders used their "authority" to direct us in what decisions to make even in our personal lives. We were drawn in more and more to the group and away from all other relationships outside the group. That included families, causing much grief.

At one point we were labeled a cult. After that, one family hired a cult expert to kidnap their loved one out of the Fellowship and debrief that person. That shocked the rest of us. We did not consider ourselves to be a cult.

When Mick began ailing, he was leading a branch of the Fellowship in another town. Our elders went to see him. Once they returned, they did not share with the rest of us Mick's situation except to say that God's judgment was falling upon him.

This non-existent explanation caused dissatisfaction. Since we knew Mick was dying of cancer, I wondered if he had changed his mind about how he and the other elders governed the Fellowship. My doubts grew stronger and when Mick passed away, I was sure he had been repenting of the direction of the Fellowship. Looking into death must make a difference in how a person sees their actions. Indeed, years later, I did hear that Mick had cried out that he had been doing the work of the devil. However, his words were hushed up at the time.

Often I felt outside the group because of my personal circumstances. My husband did not fit the mold of a man obedient to the elders dictates, and I was a working wife and mother. That did not fit the mold either. I struggled with this often. Women began wearing head coverings.

As I juggled an evolving Fellowship, a difficult home situation, and a job, God protected me. He gave me a picture one Sunday morning as I listened to a message I wasn't too sure I agreed with.

I used to do a lot of fruit and vegetable canning. I admired the colorful, luscious fruits and vegetables while strolling along aisle after aisle at the Farmer's Market trying to decide which boxes to take home. I always thought the peaches were the prettiest. Sunset colors of pinkish yellows and gold made those peaches look plump and juicy and so they proved to be when we got them home and shoved them into our mouths, sticky juice sliding down our chins.

Hot August and September afternoons steamed by as I worked in the sauna-like kitchen. My face usually rivaled the color of those peaches before I finished. Yet when I saw that bright, beautiful golden fruit in jars on my shelves, the pride of a job well done was worth the work. I knew my family would enjoy that fruit over the winter.

Sometimes before I got them all canned, I'd pick up a nice, round peach only to turn it over to see a gray fuzzy beard attached to its other side. UGH! UGH! And MORE UGH! It found its way to the trash can in a mighty hurry!

Through this analogy God taught me to immediately put to use good words that I heard, put away some words for another situation, and to throw away some words I heard altogether.

That Sunday as I listened to the message, it looked to me like it had a gray fuzzy beard, and I mentally threw it into the trash can. I reviewed the times of the Fellowship over the summer and I was agitated by much that surrounded Mick's death. The secrets, the sermons that didn't sound quite right, and the ever tighter control of "authority" were very disturbing.

At the same time, I saw my own need to control at home since life was so crazy. My anger would build quickly when situations didn't go as I thought they should. I wanted to overcome this face of anger in these adversities. Where was the victory?

Dirk, one of the elders, told me it could be a time for me to step out in faith. He was right, but not in the way he intended.

I longed to hear from Jesus. I feared not measuring up. I feared that the expectations of the Fellowship and maybe God Himself would be more than I could do. The elders talked about compromise. We weren't to do it. What was compromise? Although I'm sure this was not what they intended, I believed compromise to be the danger of being far from Jesus. This meant I must be in consistent prayer and Bible reading, regardless of what I heard in the Fellowship or anywhere else. It seemed that danger lurked no matter what I did. Seeing God's words and hearing *their* words were not always the same.

Spiritual intimidation results from not knowing where one stands with Jesus.

I wrestled with the spiritual intimidation from the Fellowship and the incomprehensible events happening at home simultaneously.

Singing in Prison

In the Book of Acts in the Bible, a story is told about how Paul and Silas were thrown into prison because of their street preaching and truth telling. The intolerable truth caused them to be shackled by chains to the walls and floors in prison. It must have been cold in there. I'm certain there were no pillows or mattresses.

We read that at midnight, the time when most of us are vulnerable to the bogey-man, they were singing and praising God. Imagine how the other prisoners might have been affected by this, maybe thinking, "Are they crazy?"

Yet suddenly, during their praise, an earthquake happened. Their chains fell off and all the doors to the prison opened. What? Sudden freedom?

The guard was ready to kill himself because he thought he had lost his prisoners, and that meant certain torture and death for him. Paul called out, "Do yourself no harm for we are all here."

The guard found a light and fell down in front of Paul and Silas, trembling. "Sirs, what must I do to be saved?" They spoke the Word of the Lord to the guard and told him to believe on the Lord Jesus Christ and he and all his household would be saved. [1]

Between my situation at home and the Fellowship, shackles from the invisible chains chafed me. I should be praising God. He was teaching me how to praise Him and wait for His deliverance from my prison. I knew an earthquake was coming. Someone in the Fellowship confirmed to me to wait for God to act as He did for Paul, Silas, and the guard. What must I do to be saved? Believe on the Lord Jesus Christ and I and all my household would be saved.

Certainly home was no haven. There lay the greatest danger and the trauma that regularly disrupted each day. No conversation with Dean could go below the surface level and, even then, he didn't remember having those conversations. I began to wonder if those discussions actually took place or if I just thought they did. Embarrassment filled me as chores were left undone, promises left unfulfilled, and bills left unpaid.

Most of all I feared for my children. I worried about what they saw and heard and if they were safe, especially when I went to work. I covered them in prayer constantly. I claimed promises from the Bible in Deuteronomy 6 that the children were sanctified as I taught them God's law and Bible stories while sitting in the house, taking walks, before bed, when we got up, and any other time. Then it would go well with them and the enemies would be shoved out.

Through prayer, I kept thrusting out the adversaries of fear, bitterness, tension, hatred, contention, big mouth, resentment, depression, and so on. I imagined my hands constantly pushing them away, but these villains relentlessly pursued my mind. If this is not prison, then what is?

Certainly the devil executed a well-planned battle strategy to ensnare me and rob me of life, joy, peace, and good nature. It was working, too. It didn't seem possible there could be a good side to life as I struggled with heartache and trouble most days.

Yet God's voice still impressed my heart. *Be patient, My daughter. Haven't I already told you that your answer is coming? You keep hearing about earthquakes. Trust Me, Child, and prepare yourself. Open your heart. I have not changed. I do not bring judgment and condemnation upon your head. Walk with Me. You have known Me in the past as a gentle guide and loving guardian. I have not changed. I love my children. Why are you listening to the lie that would tell you I am a harsh taskmaster? Turn your ears from that voice no matter from what direction it comes. I am the same yesterday, today and forever. You are safe with Me. I know your tears, I know your suffering. Your well being is at the core of My heart. I have granted the answers to those prayers of service and the knowledge of suffering. Don't turn from Me because of these extremities. Rush into my waiting arms instead. I long to hold you close. I sent My son for you. Come to Me, daughter, let Me be your refuge.*

In the darkness of the prison of those days, the comfort of an old hymn, written by Annie J. Flint, resonated with me:

He giveth more grace when the burdens grow greater;
He sendeth more strength when the labors increase.
To added affliction He addeth His mercy;
To multiplied trials, His multiplied peace.

When we have exhausted our store of endurance,
When our strength has failed ere the day is half done,
When we reach the end of our hoarded resources,
Our Father's full giving is only begun.

His love has no limit; His grace has no measure;
His pow'r has no boundary known unto men.
For out of His infinite riches in Jesus,
He giveth, and giveth, and giveth again![2]

Earthquake

When the shaking began, it was not what I expected. Is it ever? Dean's drug addiction landed him in jail for a short time. When I visited him the first night, he looked and acted like a scared child, constantly looking over his shoulders. The next night I met with him, his Mr. Tough Guy alarmed me. His whole demeanor had changed and I did not know this new person. His eyes hardened as he talked. I could see him fitting in with the other guys. Who was he?

For the first time I understood something else happening in him other than the physical injuries and drug addiction. Something mental was going on as well. I didn't know what it meant or what to do about it either, if anything, at that time.

At home the relief from tension could almost be touched. Yet other things crowded in. I left my job to stay home with the children and provide badly needed security for them. I sold possessions to keep our house and put food on the table until we all healed enough for me to get a new job. I was afraid to let the Fellowship support the kids and me because they might take over my life and then I might lose my freedom in Jesus.

I did see strength grow in my kids. Somehow God provided His own covering over them. I praised Him in gratitude.

At the same time, God showed me my own helplessness. I always thought I had such a deep constant faith in Him. Now, as teachings from the Fellowship replayed in my mind, I doubted God. What if they were right? What if God really intended me to stay in the Fellowship and I disobeyed by leaving? Could I lose my salvation after all? These weeks revealed the weakness of my faith.

Earthquake? I thought it was to be Dean's earthquake, but it shook me. Once an extrovert, I now learned doom and gloom. I faced the Cross in a new way.

As members of the Fellowship, we left family and friends behind because if God was "doing a new thing," we couldn't be held back by earthly ties. By departing, I forfeited those relationships developed within the Fellowship. Consequently, for a time, I hid away in my home. Renewing family ties and old friendships looked too big a task.

Soon after I broke from the Fellowship, Nonnie, one of the women, came to visit at my home. Her head covering and long denim skirt reminded me of the bondage I was escaping.

"So, you really are leaving?" She commented as she looked around my living room. Boxes of items were everywhere because I meant to give away some things my family no longer needed.

"Yes." I didn't want to discuss it. I knew she would report back whatever I said.

"You know you really do need to come back. That's where God placed you. Especially now that Dean is in jail." I'm sure Nonnie meant her words to be caring, but I heard judgment.

After an uncomfortable silence, she left. What a relief.

Nonnie's visit sent me to my knees again, back to the Cross. Jesus died for me and He would not leave me alone. I knew Him to be kind and loving. He doesn't say one thing and do another. The Cross is a fact.

Resurrection life follows the Cross. Life from death. This is Truth. I looked forward to the promise of assurance, joy, and laughter. My children and I could depend upon this promise even through the daily struggle. This is God's blessing, and we chose to believe it.

Dean was sentenced to several months in a drug treatment center in another city. When he left, the confusion about the Fellowship took center stage in a crisis of faith that looked like this: I once knew Jesus died and rose from the dead for me, and all I needed to do was trust Him to take me anywhere He wanted. Simple.

Now, instead of works being the natural outcome of faith; I understood through the Fellowship that I'd better do the works to make sure I kept my salvation.

As I listened to the radio one day, a dying man's voice broke into my mental fog as I heard him say that when a person looks at his own death, then he will know that the only thing that matters is clean hands and a pure heart. This stripped away my confusion.

I saw the lie in the Fellowship, though I still feared making it final and telling the leaders I would not be back.

The Juniper Tree

The prophet Elijah has always been one of my favorite Bible characters. He was so real. He gloated on the mountain top and then descended to darkest despair and moaned to God about it. Yep. I like him a lot.

In this story, Elijah just came from a huge victory at Mount Carmel with God against Queen Jezebel's Baal prophets. In a contest between God and the false gods, a big fire fell from heaven and, not only consumed the burnt sacrifice Elijah prepared, but licked up the sacrifice the false prophets attempted to offer, too.

"Cry aloud! Maybe your god is meditating—or busy—or on a trip—or even sleeping!" Elijah danced around and taunted them.

No one doubted who won that contest! The false prophets lost their lives in it.

Queen Jezebel didn't like Elijah's victory and sent him a message saying she was going to kill him. At a time when he should be trusting in God's great power, he ran, scared. He ran into the wilderness and hid under a juniper tree. He cried, "It is enough! Now, Lord, take my life, for I am no better than my fathers!" Exhaustion overwhelmed him and he lay down to sleep.

After a while, God sent him an angel with food and woke him up to eat. He ate it and went back to sleep. God sent him an angel again and fed him and told him to go on a journey.

He went to a mountain, where he listened for God's voice through a strong wind, earthquake, and fire, but did not hear God in those. It was a quiet voice that spoke to him.

"What are you doing here, Elijah?"

Elijah poured out his anguish, "I have been very zealous for the Lord God of hosts ... for the children of Israel have forsaken your covenant ... I alone am left and they seek to take my life."

God reassured him that he was not alone. God gave Elijah work to do and a friend, Elisha, to go with him. He removed the death threat.[3]

How kind and wonderful is our God, who is so gentle and loving when we are flying apart in our emotions and circumstances.

I went to my sister's house to call Dirk, the head elder at the Fellowship, to tell him I would not be coming back. He said I was running away. He said a few other things, too, that God completely wiped from my mind. This was more loving protection from the gentle hand of my Heavenly Father.

I lost friends that day and the Fellowship shunned me after that. I expected it, but standing against the disapproval of a whole group of people that I once thought loved me was not only daunting, but very hard to accept.

One afternoon as I sat in my living room, I heard a door shut in my right ear. It seemed almost audible. The door shut on old things. God provided a respite at home for my children and me. My husband went to a treatment center and would be there for several months to come. I knew a job would open up when the time was right. Finally, peace reigned for a while.

Figuratively, I sat under that juniper tree and God took gentle care of me as He did Elijah after such a great battle. The fighting was over now for a time and it was a season to rest. He even brought loving family and a new community of believers to restore my soul. God is good.

Fire and Water

Fear not the fire. I refine you through it. I will give you the desire of your heart to know Me. Walk where I set your feet looking not to the right nor to the left. I alone am He who guides your path.

These words ran through my mind as I read Isaiah 43:1–3. Our God wants the gold within us to shine forth. He will bring about all the circumstances and hard knocks to make this happen. With each hard knock, He promises to be with us through fire and water. He says we won't drown. He says we won't be burned. He says we won't even smell like smoke. He cares so much, even for how we smell after the trials! He gives us liberty in Christ: life so we can be free to tread our paths with Him, the worldly, and the unworldly. He protects us with every step in ways we don't know.

David Roper, in *Our Daily Bread*, wrote:

We may not understand why we have to endure such misery year after year. The ordeal seems endless and pointless. Our days are wasted, or so it appears. We feel as if we are doing nothing of lasting significance ... but God is doing what matters ... we are being refined ... the Refiner sits beside the crucible tempering the flames, monitoring the process, waiting patiently until His Face is mirrored in the surface.[4]

Trials don't stop as long as we live on this earth. Yet because of these two trials specifically, the Fellowship and my husband's issues, I *know* that I know that I know that God will never leave me nor forsake me. I *know* that He knows my name. I *know* that He has redeemed me forever.

One evening I prayed with my children before bed and saw behind my closed eyes a picture of a river flowing through forest and meadows. I knew it was the River of Life that flows from the Throne of God then through us and onward into the ocean of souls. We are all joined by the Spirit of God just as the earth's waterways join the oceans. God pours His living water into us, and we pour our living water into one another. May it become a mighty torrent!

CHAPTER FOUR

FAILURE AND FORGIVENESS

Growing Through Failure; Working Through Forgiveness

Yet I will not forget you. See, I have inscribed you on the palms of My hands; Your walls are continually before Me. (Isa. 49:15b–16)

Failure In The Realm

"Oh my son, Absalom! O Absalom, my son, my son!"

So King David cried when his son, Absalom, was killed in battle. The problem is that it was not in honor. Absalom was rebelling against his father, the King, and took many in the kingdom right along with him in his rebellion. A civil war was happening and it pitted king and prince against each other and tore the hearts of the people.

How did this come about? Some years before, Absalom's half brother, Amnon, took a fancy to Absalom's sister, Tamar. Evidently Amnon appeared to be wasting away in the throes of love for his half sister, and Jonadab, whom I would not call his friend, suggested that, since he was the king's son, after all, why didn't he just take her?

Amnon fell in with this idea and put into motion a plan Jonadab suggested to him which included deceived permission from his father, David, to seduce his sister forcefully. He raped her in spite of her pleadings.

Tamar's life changed dramatically. Amnon then "hated her exceedingly," so that his hatred was stronger than his love had been. She became a constant reminder of his moral failure. He threw her out of his room and she was shamed.

Her brother Absalom took her in. "Has your brother Amnon been with you? But now hold your peace, my sister. He is your brother, do not take this thing to heart." So, Tamar remained desolate in her brother Absalom's house. What brother wouldn't want to care for and protect his sister in such a situation?

When King David heard about it, he was angry but he did not do anything about it. For two years Absalom bid his time; then he concocted a scheme to get even. He, too, deceived David in order to entice his brother Amnon to a feast. He instructed his servants to kill Amnon when he was drunk. They did.

Absalom fled. When the king heard, he grieved, but wanted Absalom returned to him. David forgave him even amid palace intrigue against Absalom. One would think that Absalom would consider justice had been done for his sister Tamar.

However Absalom had nothing but contempt for his father King David. He set himself up in the gates of the city as judge in his father's place and did all manner of "in your face" kinds of things in front of his father, until open rebellion with arms broke out. The end result was a torn country and King David's grief over Absalom's death.[1]

Wow! Failure on a grand scale! I wonder how King David could forgive himself for his failure as a father and how that failure affected his entire realm.

And God called David a man after His own heart.

If Only …

Most of us aren't leading the country, and our failures don't cause civil wars. But we sure can relate to failing in our goals, our dreams, and our families. Sometimes the fear of failure is so intimidating that we don't want to take a risk at trying something our heart may long to do because of the possibility of failure. At any given time we may feel the pain of the betrayal of others as they have failed us.

When Dean's mother passed away, he was devastated. For nearly two weeks he lived in the basement family room unaware of anything around him due to his anesthetizing his pain. I waited for a time when he would be awake so I could try to help him work through the grief. One night I was on my way out the door to Bible study.

I had waited for two weeks and now all I could think of was escaping and being with people who would respond to my presence. I needed company and talking and life around me.

Just as I opened the outside door I heard this quiet little voice say, "I miss my mommy."

I hesitated. I knew I should stay. I ran.

No other time ever presented itself and I carried that failure with me for a very long time. How do you forgive yourself when you have done the unforgivable?

If only King David had spent some time with his children. How sad that such failure brought on a lack of forgiveness that it decimated a family as well as a kingdom.

If only I had gone back and spent that time with Dean when he was missing his mommy. Would it have made a difference? I grappled with forgiving myself for that failure.

How do we deal with failure? And how does failure affect forgiveness? And why do they seem to go together?

Dan Allender in *Bold Love* says, "It seems inconceivable to most of us that relief can be found in facing our failure."[2]

Relief? What a wonderful ring that sounds in our ears. Relief from our pain regardless of whether the pain is caused by ourselves or someone we thought we could trust.

He goes on to talk about running away from our own pride and self-sufficiency in order to allow God to line up our lives and relationships. How can we get out of the way and let God move into our failure?

What God has designed to be a "light burden" for us becomes heavy as we carry around our failures and unforgiveness. If only we could come to the place where we really could let Jesus carry that burden with us. Perhaps we are so hesitant to risk the letting go of those things done against us because we are afraid that justice will not be done and we won't be vindicated. Betrayal is so painful.

Most of the time we cannot do anything about how we have failed or how others have failed us. Maybe that is one of our most painful realizations. Yet if we face these failures with that knowledge, it can drive us to our knees and we go before the only One who can make any difference.

What is God Doing, Anyway?

After failure I would think, why bother? Does anybody care? Do I even care? Does God care?

"God!" I would find myself shouting. "Don't you know this is more than I can handle?" I'd be frustrated with God's seeming lack of care. After all, if He really cared, He wouldn't have allowed that to happen, right?

Am I so slow to understand? What happened to my courage to move forward and why is there such a lack of trust in God? I'm mad at God.

I tell friends that's ok. Tell God if you are mad at him. He already knows it anyway and He's big enough to take it. Now I have to face that, even though I love God with all my confused and angry heart, I am mad at Him.

How can this be? He is the One who gave Himself for me, sacrificed His life, suffered the betrayal of His friends, and set aside His glory to die for me. Yet, I am mad at Him. Can't He do something about the circumstances I endure?

I am with you; I have never left. Give yourself to Me; I want your trust. I will do mighty things in you, but I want your trust. Nothing can be accomplished unless you give yourself to Me. I need all of you, not just a part. Surrender yourself to Me. I will give you far seeing eyes, strength, and heart, but I must have all of you to fit it together or there can be nothing. The choice is yours.

The choice is mine? What does this mean? Oswald Chambers said that God cannot deliver if my interest is merely in myself. I must turn my eyes away from my hurts and fix them upon Jesus. He wants my trust and that entails surrender on my part.[3]

Before I can give forgiveness, I have to accept failure. It is unavoidable. I need to learn to walk through it and begin a journey of breaking through the bondage.

Give Me the first fruits of all your accomplishments: be they money, praise, satisfaction, people, or anything else. Give Me the dregs of your failure. I will redeem it all.

I cannot break through on my own. From *My Utmost for His Highest*, Oswald Chambers again points out that God brings crisis to our lives because we will not heed Him otherwise. Chambers continues, "If the crisis has come to you on any line, surrender your will to Him absolutely and irrevocably ... God puts you through the crisis in private, no one person can help another ... go through the crisis in will ..."[4]

This must mean I have decisions to make. God will meet me. But I meet Him, too. If I put ahead of me the goal to be like Jesus, then I cannot compare myself to others. I cannot lay expectations on others. I cannot look to performance in pleasing others. I cannot be superwoman and try to hold it all together. I cannot be responsible for anyone but myself and the results are in God's hands.

The very hands I question whether I trust. Yet if I do not take the risk, I will never know if He will come through for me or not.

In *The Healing Path*, Dan Allender paints a picture of roaming through the desert of failure.

> Damage need not destroy us! The journey of life need not strip us of joy! The walk through the desert and the valley can actually redeem us, but not if our commitment is to flee from it.[5]
>
> The desert shatters the soul's arrogance and leaves body and soul crying out in thirst and hunger. In the desert, we trust God or we die.[6]
>
> To continue to dream when failure and disappointment cloud the sun is the radical gift of hope.[7]
>
> The radical gift of hope–do we dare to reach for it?

Making Me Weak

Sandy Rios, recording artist, sings a song called "Making Me Strong." In it she sings about how she thought God was making her strong to serve Him and share His message with others. Instead, her circumstances forced her into weakness so that she might depend upon God to be her strength when she had none of her own.[8]

Scripture tells us, "Be strong in the Lord and the power of His might" (Eph. 6:10).

Sometimes we can't be strong. We are weak, with pounding hearts of fear, despair, failure, and more, but the strange thing is that we can be freed and relieved of burdens when we admit our weakness. When we admit we have no strength. We can't muster up anything to be strong. That is when our caring God takes over and gives us His strength. When we are weak, then we are strong because we find our strength in Him.

Our Father gives us rest in the midst of the journey. He holds our hands as we travel. Imagine at points along the way that your Abba Father invites you to crawl up onto His lap so He can hold you and tell you that you are His. He loves you as you are. You are His child. He will take care of you. Close your eyes and imagine His arms around you. Let your head rest against His chest. Do you hear His heart beating with His love for you? Do you feel His hand stroking your hair and His chin resting on the top of your head?

You don't have to please anyone but Me. You don't have to perform. You don't have to do anything. Be quiet in my love for you. You please Me by being yourself and coming to Me with your cares, your disappointments, your failures. I will not forget you. Your tears are safe with Me, Child.

One Size Does Not Fit All

Forgiveness is not a one size fits all. You don't just do it once and it's over. I sure wish it were that simple. Life would be so much easier. How do you forgive when it happens again and again and again? Every day. When promises aren't kept. When you carry the whole burden of the family alone. When you "lose face" in front of others. When you have to clean up situations. When you become co-dependent. When things are totally out of control.

No, forgiveness is not a one size fits all. Mourning, anger, and bitterness often filled my days as I tried to live with Dean's addictions, health issues, and mental disorder. How do you react to things you don't understand? All I could see was failure.

Dan Allender in *The Healing Path* said, "My part is to forgive on the basis of knowing I am forgiven—to bless betrayal as that which first prompts my flight from God and then reveals He is faithful, loyal, and true."[9]

I have been stung by the pain of betrayal and loss, and I found that Dan Allender is right. First I ran from God because of my anger. "It's not fair! I don't deserve it!" In realizing that part of my learning process meant remembering that sometimes I've been the one to sting, then I have to consider that maybe I do deserve it.

It was often an hourly decision to beg mercy from God and extend it to Dean. I sure didn't have any power of my own. His offenses were so *daily*, I just could not forgive him. Then I realized that *my* offenses were so daily to God and He *did* forgive me. He gave up His life on a cross to forgive me.

Daily. That word seemed to be the key. Living is a day by day experience. This kind of forgiveness had to be a daily exercise. That meant constantly going to the Cross with each offense that Dean committed against me. With each pill or each drink or each layer of attitude that came toward me from him, I would have to go to the Cross. I could not muster up forgiveness, it came from the decision to go to Jesus and lay it at His feet.

Daily. Hourly. However many times it took, through all the emotional struggles, including failure when I did it wrong.

Laying it at the feet of Jesus meant that I made a conscious effort to take those negative situations and feelings and talk to Him about them.

The first thing that usually came out of my mouth was, "God, I don't want to forgive him," and a few more words to that effect. Then I could move on to, "God, you do it for me. You know how I feel about this. I can't and don't want to forgive. I deserve better than this. You forgive for me."

God is very gracious. He knows our extremities. He knows when we think we have been pushed too far. He understands when we feel like our arms and legs are being stretched out from us in a Medieval kind of torture. Those are the times when we aren't too gracious in our demands on Him to "fix it now."

As we labor through the steps of forgiveness, we come to the place where we can say, "God! I still don't want to forgive. I still think I deserve better than this. But I want to move forward. God—please help me to be *willing* to forgive."

Nothing comes easy. Particularly if something is important for our hearts to grow and heal, it happens through a fire of some kind.

If we continue processing further, then we mature and admit, "God, I am still unwilling to forgive. But whether or not I deserve this treatment isn't as significant as pleasing You. Please give me a willing heart to forgive."

Finally the day comes when we can thank God for what He has done in our lives. The sting is finally gone. The circumstance may or may not have changed, but we realize that we really have forgiven. Perhaps over the course of working through forgiveness in this situation, we have been a part of restoring a relationship. Maybe we've had to let go of people or relationships that could not be worked out, but we let them go with peace in our hearts instead of strife, knowing that God will work out the final solutions. Future times will still come when we must "mind our minds"—that is—be vigilant to kick out the old thoughts that would come back. But with the knowledge that we have forgiven, comes the strength to resist the old thoughts.

Now we can walk forward in freedom to the next place of growth.

Yes, God is faithful, loyal, and true.

Putting On Attitudes

Developing an attitude of forgiveness was key because I knew that would be the only way I could cope with an impossible life.

"Put on tender mercies, kindness, humility, meekness, longsuffering" (Col 3:12), and "bearing with one another, and forgiving one another, if anyone has a complaint against another; even as Christ forgave you, so you must also do" (Col 3:13). I had to learn how to put on those tender mercies, the longsuffering, because I knew the same sins would occur the next day, and I would have to forgive again, even if I did not want to do it. I had to learn how to make forgiveness a lifestyle and not something I tried to do a few times. It would never "stick" those few times anyway.

I knew this: if I did not make the choice to "put on" an attitude of forgiveness, I would die inside because of bitterness. No one wants to be around a bitter, angry person. I did not want to go there.

I thought of "putting on" as I would spiritual clothing for the day. It became a daily spiritual exercise. Sometimes I succeeded and sometimes I did not, but God was always there. I was inscribed in the palm of His hand.

Letters of Forgiveness

Over the years after I left the Fellowship, I watched and I prayed as they went deeper into deception. I could not contact anyone since they would not have responded. They were closed off to the outside world. Several years went by before the day came when a child died due to lack of medical attention, a tragedy that finally broke up the group. Repercussions included jail time for some elders and other serious matters. However, most of the group were free to leave and they disbanded.

Slowly I began to contact my friends. Even through the bewilderment I saw on their faces, that I think must have mirrored my own years earlier, the joy of restoration was great.

I wrote a letter to Dirk, who had been leading the Fellowship at the time I left. Although I had settled things concerning the Fellowship with God, I still wanted to make peace with Dirk as well. He and his family moved away from the area, so I wrote him a letter offering forgiveness and asking for reconciliation.

God calls His children to live at peace with one another wherever possible. The dictionary says reconciliation means to settle a quarrel and make friendly again. In this case, where once friendship existed, a rift went deep. A few months passed and I wondered if Dirk and his family were just putting everything behind them. Then one day I found a letter in the mailbox. Even though Dirk, his family, and mine have not seen each other since then, reconciliation did happen through those two letters and closure was possible. The old deceptions were addressed and forgiven and the road to follow God was clear. On both sides. God is good.

Redeemed Failure

King David's sons, Absalom and Amnon, could never be brought back. Nor could Tamar's life before her devastation be restored. My own story concerning that night when I left Dean alone missing his mommy cannot be changed this side of heaven, but I look forward to that forgiveness from Dean in heaven. For now I will rest it at the foot of the Cross. Only God can take care of things that are beyond us. This is part of redemption.

God is faithful to handle injustice when we take it to Him—in forgiving people we can't seem to forgive, or forgiving ourselves for doing the unforgivable. The Cross is the leveler. Jesus will make it right in our souls and for all eternity. We are freed from having to understand.

Later in the story, we see King David spending time instructing his son and heir, Prince Solomon. God was gracious to give him another opportunity to redeem the throne of Israel with a godly presence.

"Then the days of David drew near that he should die, and he charged Solomon his son, saying, I go the way of all the earth; be strong, therefore, and prove yourself a man. And keep the charge of the Lord your God: to walk in His ways, to keep His statutes, His commandments, His judgments, and His testimonies ... that the Lord may fulfill His Word which He spoke concerning me, saying, 'If your sons take heed to their way, to walk before Me in truth with all their heart and with all their soul … you shall not lack a man on the throne of Israel'" (I Kings 2:1–4).

This time, when God gave David another son, David did not waste that life. He spent time with Solomon instructing him in the ways of God and in the ways of living as a king in a godly realm. The result is that King Solomon, when asked by God what he wanted, requested wisdom to rule his people. He is known as the wisest man who ever lived.

How is that for redemption of failure?

A Walk Pleasing God

Failure and forgiveness are two of the most difficult areas to move through in our lives. Both of these are accompanied by circumstances and emotions that seem to be impossible and we wonder if we can ever rise above them. No easy answers come to mind. Sometimes, as we have seen and even experienced, it takes years to walk through.

We do have the promises of God and the opportunity to call upon the people around us for support. As we search out God, He is pleased with us. Even when we find it hard to believe that He has good things for us, His Word assures us that it is true.

The first chapter of Colossians gives me much encouragement. If I read God's instructions every day and allow my spirit to be filled with the knowledge of God's will, with wisdom and spiritual understanding, then I will have a "walk, worthy of the Lord, fully pleasing Him." I claim the promise that I will be fruitful in all I do. I will increase in the knowledge of God. I will be strengthened with His might and power. I will have patience, long suffering, and joy. I will be an heir of His kingdom and I will be fully thankful for His deliverance from all the powers of darkness.[10]

Jesus made all of this possible for us. He made life something we can do with hope even in hopeless circumstances. Even through failure and forgiveness.

I am with you; I have never left. Give yourself to Me.

As we go to our knees and face the depths of our hearts on the discomfort of the floor before God, He meets us there. He is eager to meet us there. For without Him life cannot hold sustaining energy, excitement or abundance. He has promised that kind of life to those who will seek Him as they would for treasure. Like an obsession?

Ah—but He is obsessed with us! "Today, when you hear His Voice, do not harden your hearts" (Heb. 3:7, 8).

CHAPTER FIVE

FEAR AND SOUND MIND

An Introduction to Spiritual Warfare

For God has not given us a spirit of fear, but of power, and of love and of a sound mind. (2 Tim. 1:7)

I've lived my life in a war zone. All of us have, but most of us do not realize it. At some point, I realized that there is a war to fight in the heavenly realm that directly affects my affairs on earth.

We Can't Wake Daddy Up!

After calming my children the night I came home from work to find them hysterical and trying to wake up their father, I had my own trauma to conquer. When I saw his sightless eyes staring upward, I froze.

In unreasoning fear, I called a friend, "Joan! Pray now! I think Dean might be dying this time!"

Then I flung the phone down and dropped to the floor, burying my face in my arms in front of Dean as he lay in his chair. The TV droned in front of us, but I didn't hear anything but my own terror.

"God! Do something! Please don't let him die tonight!" I sobbed. I couldn't wake Daddy up either. Only God could do that now.

For two hours I lay before God crying out. Then Dean moved his little finger and, from previous experiences in watching him, I knew he was going to be all right. Fifteen minutes later he got up and went to bed. I still sat on the floor.

I grappled with what had happened. It horrified me that I had not called 911! What was I thinking? Yet because of God's mercy and grace through my intercession and my friend's prayers, Dean lived. Relief wasn't a big enough word to cover my feelings.

The next day when I brought up what had happened, Dean admitted that he remembered floating above his body and being terrified because he didn't know how to get back into it.

After this occurrence I became aware of another world superimposed on the one we see and feel and touch. I also became afraid of that world. Without God's power through the Blood of Jesus Christ and His Name, we are helpless. But because He has given us Himself, we have all authority. We need to learn what that means and how to make it work when that "other world" invades the one we can see, feel, and touch.

It's War

This ordeal started me down a new path. Fear became a way of life. What would I find every time I came home and walked through the door? I thought I was losing my sanity. For the first time in my life I felt I was going down and couldn't get up again. I saw myself on a cliff, grasping frantically at grass or roots, or anything, for a firm hold. My arm and part of my body was hanging over the edge and Dean was clutching me as he dangled in the air. Below were rocks and death.

Since we are drafted into spiritual war, we all come to the place where we decide if we are going to be shot and lay on the battlefield, or are we going to pick up our armor and stand and fight? This was my reality as I stared down that cliff.

A new element entered into my thinking. God really *does* care about our everyday affairs. He is keenly interested in us. So is the devil.

The Bible, God's Word, tells us that Jesus came to defeat all the enemies of our souls. We are given armor in God's Word, in Ephesians 6:10–18. We are told to put it on. As we put it on, we have the power of God to stand. Why do we need it? Our enemies are spiritual beings bent on our destruction. Why is that? Because of the love that God bears us. We are pawns in a spiritual vendetta.

The armor is a picture of the Roman military "uniform." The Helmet of Salvation protects our minds, the Belt of Truth gives us confidence, the Breastplate of Righteousness protects our hearts and vital organs, the Shoes of Good News give us a sure path to follow, the Shield of Faith allows us to advance as it takes the arrows aimed at us, and the Sword of the Spirit, which is God's Word, gives us victory as we learn to wield it.

We are then told to stand and withstand the wiles of the devil.[1]

I don't think "wiles" begins to describe how this war seizes our souls. Sometimes it feels like we have been caught in a whirlpool, spinning around and around. Satan's jaws seem to be yawning down the vortex of that pool. We somehow drift to the side of the pool looking for relief, but are grabbed again by the merciless waves of turmoil. But we don't have to stay in that whirlpool because God made a way by sending us His son, Jesus, to lift us out. Then He's given us armor so we can stand and fight.

I soon noticed that the battles I found myself facing were not random, but systematic attacks on my soul. I didn't have a choice whether or not I wanted to be in this war and no amount of running away would get me out of it. Not only that, but I was discovering I was not the only one in this war. As long as we are here on earth, we will encounter battles to fight in our everyday lives. We need each other in community as we hold each other up. This made sense to me as life was unfolding in all its desperation.

People came alongside me in different seasons and situations. Some were good listeners. Some prayed with me. Some had practical helps to offer me. Some were professional counselors. Because of community, doors of understanding and knowledge opened up for me and I realized that we must stand and fight in this war together.

I am constantly learning about spiritual warfare. Certain moments are prime time for God to work in an individual's life. Two Greek words illustrate this. Something that is well-timed or an opportunity just ready to happen is "kairos." This is different from "chronos" time, which is measurable time: minutes, hours, etc.

Dutch Sheets, in his book, *Intercessory Prayer*, discusses this and a Hebrew word for intercession, "paga." "Paga" has several meanings, two of which interested me. One of these is to meet and a second is boundaries. Dutch Sheets said, "Intercession creates a meeting. Intercessors meet with God; they also meet with the powers of darkness." At one point in his book, he describes "paga" as a violent meeting between light and darkness; much like the force of a lightning bolt as it slams to the earth with sparks of light.[2]

The Dunamis Course, from the ministry of Presbyterian-Reformed Ministries International, talks about "kairos" time in connection with God working in love relationships; faith opening the door for the work of God as the intercessor meets with God and God is ready to act.[3]

As I learned about "kairos" time and "paga," and God acting when the intercessor (the person who prays) comes before Him on behalf of another, I began to understand what happened that night that my children could not "wake Daddy up."

It is not God's plan that anyone should be lost in eternity. Dean was very close that night to eternity without God. What a frightful place to be!

God was ready to act for Dean. However, He needed an earthly intercessor to meet with Him on Dean's behalf in that "kairos" time and pray for a boundary of protection, "paga," around Dean so that He could do a work for Dean. I did not understand what was happening at the time. All I knew was that I had to call my friend to pray, and get on my own face before God to desperately pray for Dean's soul.

I could not see the fierce battle taking place for Dean during that "paga," but I believe that God was just as desperate to answer that prayer so that this one sheep would not be lost to Him forever. Dean lived that night and for several more years. In that "kairos" moment, God taught my arms to make war. The enemy lost that battle.

Psalm 18 is a psalm of war. It talks about God being our strength, our fortress, our rock, deliverer, shield, horn of salvation, and stronghold. He is worthy of our praise and our love. When we call on Him, He saves us from our enemies.

It goes on to say how angry He is on our behalf and thunders until the very foundations of the world are uncovered. He will spare nothing to come to our aid.

He teaches us how to make war. As we acknowledge Him as God and the one who arms us with strength, He sets our feet in a place of victory. We overcome our spiritual enemies. The necks of those spiritual enemies are exposed to us.[4]

In Joshua 10, it describes how the enemies are laid out and their necks stretched. The foot of the victor is placed on the neck and with a quick stroke of a sword, the enemy is slain (Josh. 10:24–26). This is the final vanquishing of the enemy, made possible by the Cross of Christ, and we are given His victory. How gracious is our God!

Heroic Faith

In *My Utmost For His Highest*, Oswald Chambers says, "Faith is the heroic effort of your life, you fling yourself in reckless confidence on God."[5]

God calls us to heroic efforts in this war. We didn't ask to sign up to be a soldier. It is an automatic induction when we are born into this world. We become special targets when we come to saving faith in Jesus Christ.

Oftentimes we are bewildered and beleaguered soldiers. Sometimes we fall. Sometimes we despair. Always we need to fight for and with our community. We may think that we should muster up some kind of special faith, and we fall short. We forget that our God is with us all the time. He doesn't ask for grandiose actions, He simply wants us to call on Him and trust that He will be with us. This includes big or little situations.

In 2 Kings, we read a story of God's protection during a war scenario. As often happened, a conflict was in progress between the King of Syria and the King of Israel. The King of Israel sought the counsel of the Man of God, Elisha the Prophet. Since the plans of the Syrian king were often foiled, he decided to go after Elisha. He sent an army to the town where Elisha and his servant dwelled, and they surrounded the city.

Elisha's servant woke up the next morning and saw the army. He panicked with fear and ran to Elisha, crying, "Alas, my master! What shall we do?"

Elisha was not moved. He calmly answered, "Do not fear, for those who are with us are more than those who are with them." Then he prayed and asked God to open the spiritual eyes of his servant to see.

The servant looked around and saw a much greater army upon the mountains around them. The chariots of this army were of fire!

Elisha prayed for blindness for the Syrian army then he led them to the King of Israel who, at Elisha's command, had mercy on them. The king fed them. Elisha prayed for their restored sight and they were sent home to their own king. They never returned.[6]

What an amazing story. To think that God surrounds us with His army that is much greater than any army that comes against us. I believe that if I saw chariots of fire coming at me, I would be on my face begging for mercy.

Another time when I came up against that other world of war, I had a job that required me to make weekly deliveries to a business in the downtown area. This day I parked my car and began the walk to the crosswalk as usual. I noticed a commotion across the street from where I stood. A middle-aged woman was striding through moving traffic and shouting expletives as she went. The light changed for me and I began to cross the street.

I could see that I was going to get to the corner right behind her. I slowed my pace. I did not want to be too close. She was still shouting. I followed her for half a block. As we approached the courtyard where I would have to make a turn into the building, I hoped she would continue on her way. But no, she entered the courtyard. She headed to the same place where I was going.

Without warning, something turned her around to face me. I stopped. I was scared.

"Are you following us?" Came the gravelly inquiry from her mouth. Her face was malevolent. I can't think of any other way to say it.

I responded in my mind with these words, "Ok, Lord, it's you and me." I couldn't think of anything else but I guess it was enough.

She turned around again and proceeded forward, shouting once more just as if I was not there.

Curiously I looked over my shoulder. I wondered if I would see an army of angels behind me. I didn't, but I am sure, like Elisha, that there were more with me than with that poor woman.

That day I learned God answers our calls instantly. Even if we don't do it right because we don't know what is right. He promises us in His Word that when we call, He will answer. I could see that He does. He responds to our heroic efforts of faith.

Power by the Hour

But what if He doesn't answer instantly? Many of us live with constant "what ifs" that never happen, and with some that do happen. We are helpless in the face of fear. The fight against panic is a constant battle. We struggle to keep a sound mind as we face the giants in our lives.

Often it's a waiting game over the course of living before we can understand the answers to our prayers. Maybe those answers aren't what we want. Frequently, it's through much time, turmoil, and groaning before we see an answer come.

I used to wonder what today would bring. The future could not be contemplated because today was so difficult to get through.

In the Old Testament, Daniel was a prophet who prayed for an answer. He fasted and mourned for his answer. When it finally came, it was explained to him that the answer had been sent immediately but the messenger got caught in a battle on his way to Daniel (Dan. 10:12–13). There is that unseen war again. How many times does it change the course of human events? How many times does it change the course of our very own lives?

We pray out of our desperation and when the answer is delayed, we think God has not heard us. Or if the answer is not what we hoped, we think that God does not care.

What we don't understand is that God is eager to act on our behalf. We want to box Him into our ideas of love, goodness, and wisdom when all the time it is God alone who knows all truth, is everywhere, and can do all things. He always does what is best for us.

Still, a war rages around us and would hinder the good things in store for us. Here we are, soldiers inducted to engage, and our weapons are as unseen as the war we fight. We must remember to put on our spiritual armor.

As we have learned, part of that armor is the Helmet of Salvation. Checking first to be sure that our commander is Jesus, we then check our thought life. The Bible tells us, "For the weapons of our warfare are not carnal but mighty in God for pulling down strongholds, casting down imaginations and every high thing that exalts itself against the knowledge of God, bringing every thought into captivity to the obedience of Christ" (2 Cor. 10:4, 5).

Figuring out which thoughts to keep and reject must be one of the most difficult things we do, and it is constant. Our minds are always going to and fro with something.

For a period of time fear was my persistent companion. I didn't want it around, but I seemed powerless to rise out of it. I stopped on my way home from work every night to sit in my car and pray before coming home. Those most important moments gave me the courage to face whatever was at home that night. I heard God speak to my spirit as the conflict continued in my life. Sometimes I could feel the rage and desperation of the devil boiling around me. Sometimes I'd win, and sometimes he'd win, but the devil could never be the final victor!

Filling my mind with scripture verses every minute was imperative or I would be dwelling on emotional traumas or traumas happening in my external world.

One of the passages I read was Exodus 14. Moses was leading the Israelites away from Egypt, and they had come up against the Red Sea. By this time, the Egyptians were coming after them. There was no place for them to go. I thought there was no place for me to go either. I read further. I saw that there would be death for the Israelites either way.

The sea roared on one side and a vengeful king with soldiers out to kill them was on the other side. God spoke directly to their immediate problem and told them not to fear, but to stand still and see what He would do to deliver them. He did a *big thing*. He parted the sea! What? That's impossible! He drowned the Egyptians behind them. He completely saved them. What would He do for me when I came up against the seas and soldiers in my life?

I faced issues at home that meant I needed power by the hour. I sensed the presence of those unseen spiritual beings intent on my destruction, and fear of them put me into a POW camp for years. Waves and waves of fear hit me. At times I felt nearly incapable of functioning, so great was the fear. I constantly read the Bible and prayed. I did all I knew to do to abide in Christ. I really had to learn to believe God no matter how I felt and what was happening around me. Sometimes I thought I would slip over the edge into insanity, so unbearable were the panic attacks.

Spiritual darkness surrounded me and it felt like something pressed on me from all sides. I imagined I could hear raucous laughter. I determined to go through by trusting God. Through much Bible reading, I had assurance that God would not leave me. He would save and protect my children, even teach them and prosper them, and that His words would not depart from their mouths forever.

How did I get sprung from this trap?

First, the trap door opened through faith in the power of God to deliver. I had to make a conscious decision to believe what I read. I found that He is faithful and if He said He would stay with me, then He would. He said when we call, He will answer. He does. Faith is hard when God can't be seen or felt with your hands, but He never leaves us alone, no matter what.

Second, He gave me a wonderful, loving community. This included those in the professional community. As I interacted with these dear friends and family, they encouraged me to trust God through waiting and continuing to believe what I read in the Bible even through contrary circumstances. They shared their prayer support with me as well as their knowledge and experience. They waited with me.

Third, I had to make determined efforts to get rid of the dark thoughts as they came. That's when I usually ran for my Bible. God's Word strengthens the shield of faith and it *is* the sword, after all!

No darkness is too dark for God to penetrate! No darkness of mind is too great for Him. He restores our souls. I found that out of such oppression comes a cry of anguish and all other things are squeezed out except the longing for God, and He is there.

I learned a few other things as well. In trying to understand this battle, I came to see that the Holy Spirit is the *real power* over all. No created thing can overcome its Creator. That includes the unseen beings in opposition to us. I learned to pray always. We must be persistent through the battle because the devil is persistent. He's had centuries of practice, too. So we must be *more* persistent. We have the Holy Spirit's power, and the devil must flee as we lean into God.

Did my circumstances change then? No. My focus changed and I was freed from the fear. But it didn't happen in a day.

Fear is crazy making. Things sound normal that are not normal. Fear makes us act on ideas that are not true. Fear makes us want to run away instead of standing strong. Fear paralyzes us when danger comes from without or within.

"I'm so scared. Your Word says you have not given us a spirit of fear, but of love, power, and sound mind. I need your power, God! I need your sound mind! I need your love! Show me how to battle these powers in my home."

God provides a sound mind for us. Mental health comes from attitudes, choices, and taking care of our bodies and minds. Getting rest physically will refresh our bodies. To choose what we will allow to linger in our minds will alter the course of our attitudes. Set those "eye and ear gates" toward positives. Think on those things.

Scott Peck said, "Mental health is the ongoing process of dedication to reality at all costs."[7] In light of this, I think that mental sickness must be the running away from reality at all costs.

If seeking mental health means to seek professional help, then run, don't walk. Only God knows the intricacies of our minds, but He provides communities and endows them with gifts to help one another where it is needed. Sound mind sometimes may mean taking yourself out of a situation temporarily or permanently. Sound mind *always* means going to God on your knees.

Fear Not! Sound Mind Belongs to the Steadfast

We don't have to live with fear because, if Jesus has saved us, then we are covered by His Name and His Blood. Oppression has no place in us.

We have power through the Blood of the Lamb.

We have love because Jesus loves us and gave Himself for us.

We have a sound mind because it's clear and washed clean, and we can absorb God's Word for our protection.

We are free to worship the God who loves us. The antithesis of fear is worship and delight. How can God delight in our worship of Him if we are in fear and not delighting in Him? He longs for us to delight in Him. Go ahead and sing at the top of your lungs and dance. Let the spirits of darkness hear it and shudder.

How good God is! All the time, and no matter what.

CHAPTER SIX

KEEPING ON VS. COMMON SENSE

Learning to Lean on God

I would have lost heart, unless I had believed that I would see the goodness of the Lord in the land of the living. Wait on the Lord; be of good courage, and He shall strengthen your heart; wait, I say, on the Lord! (Ps. 27:13, 14)

Weeping may endure for a night, but joy comes in the morning. (Ps. 30:5)

Call of God

"I have finally realized that nothing is going to change. It's always going to be this way. Dean isn't going to get better and I need to face that the rest of my life may be spent dealing with all this."

My counselor, leaning back in his chair, pushed his pen and pad across his lap and silently regarded me.

"We've tried a lot of treatments," he agreed after a few moments. "He has to be willing to work with us. This is a last resort but have you thought of leaving him?"

"Every day," I responded promptly. "But God said 'no.'"

Again, he gazed at me silently. "Sometimes, for your own sake, this is an option. Unless there is a specific call of God to see it through ..."

Something in my face must have alerted him for he sat up straight and pulled his pen and pad toward him. "All right, then. Going on the premise that this is a permanent situation, let's see how we can keep you sane and best help Dean in spite of himself."

"Sanity would be good," I said fervently. "I would like that a lot."

God's Perseverance

I am struck that God persevered in calling the prophet Samuel. When Samuel was a boy, at the beginning of his ministry, God called him in the middle of the night. Three times Samuel ran to his master, Eli, and said, "Here I am, for you called me."

Three times Eli answered, "I did not call you. Go back to bed."

The fourth time the call came, Scripture says, "Then the Lord came and stood and called ..."[1]

What was that? God came and stood and called?

Would God do that for anybody? Would He do that for me?

This came to my notice from part of a sermon delivered by Pastor Steve Flora, who served at Garland Alliance Church in Spokane, Washington. Pastor Steve grabbed my attention as he told the story of young Samuel's first calling as prophet by God in 1 Samuel 3. I immediately thought of the conversation with my counselor concerning the call of God. So my ears were tuned this day.

Pastor Steve had several points to his sermon that I jotted down. He talked about starting with a servant's heart. We die to our own agendas and put others above ourselves. We listen to hear God's call, then we let go. This might mean a "forced growth" in our souls. Finally, we do what God has called us to do, and He causes us to do it well.

Samuel was young and he was ready to serve his teacher, Eli. When the Word of the Lord came to Samuel, he answered quickly. Eli, perceiving it was God, told Samuel to pay attention. He obeyed. As Pastor Steve said, "God had found a servant whom He could entrust to apply his Word to real life—these "here I ams" demonstrate that Samuel was willing to honor Eli as his elder."

What about listening to hear God's call? That God would actually come and stand and call is a fascination to me. Can He really be so eager for us to follow Him? Pastor Steve said, "The Lord's repetition of Samuel's name added a note of urgency. Samuel's response was to say, 'Your servant is listening.' Listen means to hear so as to obey. The person who surrenders to the Lord and is willing to listen will always learn God's will." I concluded that if I put myself into an attitude of open quietness before God, then He would come.

Next God pressed Samuel to give Eli a hard word. Samuel had been raised as a son by Eli and now God chose Him to inform Eli that his time, and that of his wicked sons, was finished. Through a time of "forced growth," as Samuel must have agonized over this confrontation and finally obeyed in delivering it, a new era entered. Now, as Pastor Steve put it, "Samuel had found his calling and he was willing to go!"

That led into the next point of doing what God has called us to do and do it well. Pastor Steve had this to say, "Discovering our God destiny, our divine calling, is the most important task of our lives. All of our God destinies are about learning to know God more intimately. But God has a unique design for how that will look in our lives. Samuel had a prophetic calling. Your calling will draw you to God, but may have a different flavor."

A "different flavor." Well yes, I think so.

For me that "different flavor" looked like perseverance. God was calling me to stand in the gap for Dean and for my family.

The Gap

The prophet Isaiah overheard God calling out, "Go and tell this people: Keep on hearing, but do not understand; Keep on seeing, but do not perceive. Make the heart of this people dull, And their ears heavy, And shut their eyes; Lest they see with their eyes, And hear with their ears, And understand with their heart, And return and be healed" (Isa. 6:9, 10). Isaiah's response was, "Lord, how long?"

It seems to me that God kept looking for prophets in the Old Testament to go stand in the gap and pray even if results were negative or things got worse. The prophet Jeremiah cried all the time. I can understand that. No one would listen to his messages.

Persevering. Standing in the gap. That is *so* against the stream! Today we are trained to put ourselves first. We are all looking for someone to love us but few of us want to *be* the person who does the loving. It requires too much from us. What kind of upheaval does it take for us to completely change our minds and answer God's call to stand in the gap for another?

God tells us repeatedly to trust Him, to look for Him to come in a situation, to believe that He will see us through. It takes a glimpse of the bigger picture. If we are to pursue being like Jesus, then standing in the gap for the sake of others is part of our "reasonable service."

Yet even as things worsen, we can look up and rejoice because our redemption draws near. We continue on in prayer no matter what the outcome.

Hosea's Prostitute

Hosea married a prostitute. The Old Testament records his story. Gomer, the wife God chose for Hosea, constantly ran off after other lovers. Hosea constantly went after her to bring her home and restore her. She had children by these lovers and Hosea named them after the sin that spawned them.[2]

This picture of Hosea's love for a faithless wife struck through my life with a force that pierced. God was calling me to do the same for Dean. His wandering soul chose to run away and hide rather than fight through to the victory.

Dean's "lovers" were drugs, alcohol, creature comforts, and food, and he had impenetrable mental "layers" that made it impossible to relate to him. He was very complicated and darkness and despair hung about him like draperies.

Hosea lived with darkness and despair. I think I know how he felt. I came to understand that this was the role God had chosen for me. As Hosea was to remain faithful to Gomer in order to model God's faithfulness to His beloved but faithless people, so was I to model God's faithfulness to Dean. If I stayed in spite of Dean's "lovers," then Dean would understand on some level that God was his Father and would never leave him.

I once wrote in a journal, "Dean pretends so well. Sometimes I wonder if anybody is home inside his head? Is his soul stuffed so tightly away that he can't reach it anymore?" I worried about his mental state.

I used to say that Perseverance was my middle name. I said it with a sigh. I didn't know then about my life being part of a bigger plan. I just knew that living this way was painful but I was supposed to keep going.

I didn't know God would come and stand and call me to Himself. I didn't know how passionate and eager He is to interact with us. I didn't know that if I choose to trust Him willingly, He will come through for me and He will do it *big!*

Oswald Chambers, in *My Utmost for His Highest*, said,

We need to rely on the resurrection life of Jesus much deeper than we do, to get into the habit of steadily referring everything back to Him. We are not told to walk in the light of conscience or of a sense of duty, but to walk in the light as God is in the light. When we do anything from a sense of duty, we can back it up by argument; when we do anything in obedience to the Lord, there is no argument possible; that is why a saint can be easily ridiculed.[3]

I learned to take each day as it came, enjoy what I could, and leave tomorrow in God's hands. I worried that I was living in unreality. Where did the line divide between facing reality and dealing with it or leaving things in God's hands?

I had to be prepared for ridicule, to walk in the plan that God had laid out for me even though it seemed senseless and pointless. What kind of person puts herself in this kind of situation and stays? Would it look like something was wrong with me? How would I be perceived by others? Living this way was totally against the prevailing common sense.

Believing Truth In Perseverance

The place where perseverance finds strength is in persistent prayer. Such a force of the enemy surrounded Dean and our family. The heavy fog hung so dense that the dangers could not even be seen. It felt like Jack the Ripper stalked the streets and I never knew when he might rush out at me with his dagger. When would deliverance come?

The struggle was taking so long and so many routes that my head and heart whirled with hazy confusion most of the time.

I clung to the knowledge that *God always sees me!*

If the warfare delays the answer, does that make God less powerful? No! We gave Satan the right of rule in this world when we gave up our right of dominion in the Garden of Eden.

That's the old story in Genesis when God made a man and a woman to rule over all the beasts, birds, and all the earth. He gave

His new creation His beauty, His love, and His companionship. The only thing He withheld from them was the fruit of the Tree of the Knowledge of Good and Evil. Well, everything was fine for a while. Fine, that is, until the serpent let the devil work through him to fool Adam and Eve into eating of the fruit. The self-satisfied devil slithered away and devastation ruled instead of Adam and Eve. God, in His justice, had to curse them, the serpent, and the earth. Death entered in, as well as all manner of evil things. The man and woman no longer ruled the earth.

So even Satan benefits because of God's justice and enjoys the rule of this world for an appointed amount of time. But for *only* an appointed amount of time. After that he will be vanquished.[4]

Before sending the man and woman out of the garden, God promised them redemption. His Word is good. He sent His Son, Jesus, to die on the cross, rise from the dead, and give us victory. Even now. We don't have to wait for the vanquishing of the devil, for it is already done for us when we believe Jesus.

We may still have to fight through the fog. We may still have Jack the Ripper rushing us unexpectedly from all sides—but we will win as we depend upon God who has made a way for us. We have His strength in our weakness.

I continued to put on my armor.

One night stands out as I was going to bed at my brother and sister-in-law's home. God impressed me to pray earnestly for Dean. I wondered if he was dying that night, so strong was the impression. He didn't die then. I found out later that my nephew, Dan, had also been impressed to pray for his Uncle Dean that night. When we compared notes, we found it was the same time—11:15 PM.

Perseverance in prayer. These are the weapons of our warfare in force. Armed conflict takes time and it wears us down. But if we believe God has given the victory and we draw on His strength to keep going, then we will see it. He's already given it.

Hidden Valleys

During a difficult period of time when we tried to get Dean into treatment, I spent a couple weeks staying with family members. Dean wasn't happy about the situation but we were trying to save his life since his addictions had slipped so far.

A few times I talked to him on the phone, and my sister-in-law said afterward, "You talk to him like he's a child." My response to her was, "he *is* a child." At this time we saw several sides to him. He would threaten to do things but he never followed through. I called my counselor several times a day for a while. I made a lot of trips home to check on Dean, the cats, or the property. My grown children had married and were living their own lives in their own homes in other states.

During this stressful season, I held on to Kelly Willard's words in her song *Hidden Valleys*. She wrote about how the hidden valleys of our lives produce strength and how desperation has a song at its outcome. Shepherds become kings because of the suffering they endure in the valleys of their souls.[5]

It reinforced for me how character is shaped in the hidden places as we surrender our wills. We praise God in the middle of those lonely seasons when we face the storms that rampage against us, and God meets us there.

Abigail's Story

Abigail's story from 1 Samuel 25, outlines wonderfully how character is developed in hidden valleys. Through Abigail we can see how God works in those who allow Him to take them through the dark times of life.

Her good sense and beauty were well known, but her husband, Nabal, was known for his harshness and evil foolishness.

In those days in Israel, shepherds cared for their master's sheep. We would say "employers" today. The shepherds were guarded in their work by roving bands of young men who earned their living by providing this protection. It worked well. Most of the time the guards and the shepherds formed trusting friendships.

When the time for shearing the sheep arrived, it was expected that the sheep owner would compensate the young men with food and goods for the services they had rendered.

This story opens at sheep shearing time. David sent ten of his young men to collect their compensation from Nabal. The young men greeted Nabal with blessings at David's instructions.

"Peace be to you and your house and all you have ... we guarded your shepherds and we did not hurt them, nor was there anything missing from them ... ask them ... they will tell you ... let my young men find favor in your sight ... please give whatever comes to hand ..."

In other words they blessed Nabal, gave him a report, and left the compensation open handed, that is, up to Nabal's discretion.

Nabal answered, "Who is David? ... Shall I give away ... my goods to young men that I do not know where they are from?" He insulted them in a very ugly manner. So ugly that they "turned on their heels" and returned to David with their report.

David flamed with anger.

"Every man gird on his sword!"

David was ready to slaughter everyone in Nabal's employ whom he had just spent months guarding. His young men were now on the march.

Meanwhile, back at the ranch, a servant went to Abigail, Nabal's wife, and told her what happened. He stressed that David's men had been good to them and guarded them well day and night.

"Now, therefore, know and consider what you will do ... harm is determined against our master and all his household ... he is such a scoundrel that one cannot speak to him."

The Bible says that Abigail wasted no time in putting together a huge amount of goods and food and sending them on the backs of several donkeys to meet David and his men en route. She, herself, followed it.

As she met David, she slipped off her mount and "fell on her face before David and bowed to the ground." She cried out for forgiveness and pled for the lives of all Nabal's household. "Please let not my lord regard this scoundrel … Nabal is his name and folly is with him."

She appealed to David's godliness in reminding him that he was God's chosen king and that he would not want to begin ruling a nation with murder on his hands due to revenge.

David relented, accepted her gifts, lifted her up, and blessed her. "Go up in peace to your house. See, I have heeded your voice and respected your person." He would remember her.

Abigail returned home to find a drunken Nabal partying. She told him nothing of what had happened until the next morning. She did not know how Nabal might react to her news. When she did tell him, Nabal suffered a heart attack and died shortly after.

When David heard that Abigail had been widowed, he sent for her. She immediately called for her maids and went with David's messengers. He married her and she became the mother of a son of David.[6]

Abigail, My Model

When I first came across Abigail's story, I thought what a good model she could be for me. She was married to a man who was incapable of dealing with his life. He looked like an alcoholic to me. He was verbally abusive and had nothing to do with the values of God. Those things were evident in how he treated his household and how he treated those who had done a great service for him.

In that culture a woman could not be independent very easily. Her husband was chosen for her and if he died, she did not inherit his wealth. It went to a male relative. A woman alone was suspect.

In these circumstances, Abigail's character shines. She persevered. Even as she recognized the truth, "Nabal is a fool," she ran her household with grace and encouragement. She did not descend into useless depression or self pity. She set about making a home and caring for those within the household.

In turn, those of Nabal's estate respected and loved Abigail. It is significant that the servant came directly to her when Nabal blew off David's young men and brought trouble down upon all their heads. The servant not only spoke frankly to her but he was not afraid to voice his opinion of Nabal to her. Then he trusted her to right the wrong.

Abigail was a shrewd businesswoman as shown by the way she flew into action when she learned of the impending danger. I can imagine her barking out orders, "You—get two hundred loaves of bread ready to go! You—I need two skins of wine out in the yard pronto! You—those five sheep over there that are dressed and ready for roasting, package them and load them up! You—grab those bags of roasted grain; load them up behind the sheep! You—over there, the clusters of raisins and the cakes of figs, they go, too! Everyone, hurry! We don't have much time! We'll need to meet our guards on the road—let's go—NOW!"

Abigail was ready to do whatever was necessary when evil was present. Even when her circumstances were unfair to her. She determined she would live her life to glorify God and to do right no matter what came her way. Her reward came in the love and respect that she received from those she served as mistress on Nabal's estate. I believe she must have had a thriving faith and love for God to persevere as she did.

When Nabal died, Abigail lost the entire life she had been living. It must have been difficult for her to realize that she had nowhere to go and would soon be no longer welcome in the home she had ruled over.

Then came David's proposal, and the Scripture says, "She rose in haste and rode on a donkey attended by five maidservants."

With my modern day mindset, I thought Abigail had jumped from the frying pan into the fire by going with David. After all, he had other wives and concubines, too. Why would she want to do that?

After careful thought, I have come to the conclusion that this was, indeed, a reward for her. A woman could not inherit property. That prospect was reserved for the nearest male relation. That would mean Nabal's nearest relation. Abigail would be homeless unless that male relative allowed her to live there. Furthermore, the custom of the day decreed that the male relative could marry the widow and provide an heir for her to carry on the family line. What if he already had other wives? Abigail also would give up running the household that she had ruled for years. I would think she probably had enough of Nabal's family and took the way of escape offered to her through David.

Through marriage, David offered her a home. He offered her a position within the framework of that society. She bore a son to David. A barren woman was not respected in that culture, barrenness meant shame. As one of the King's wives and the mother of one of the King's sons, Abigail would be very honored. We already know that David admired and respected her, and I think he set out to make sure her life would be comfortable.

I think they were always friends and I like to think that David consulted Abigail on affairs of State now and then, since her good sense was so well known. I am sure there must have been some important work she did in the kingdom. It would seem to be in character for her.

I could not think of a better woman to model my life after than this woman who persevered through difficult circumstances, cared for those around her, kept a wary guard over her attitudes, and acted when necessary in the face of danger—even to risking a frightening outcome.

Persevering Through Twisted Thinking

One chapter in *Bold Love*, written by Dan Allender and Dr. Tremper Longman, considers loving the fool.[7] The fool is the one who says in his heart, "There is no God," and lives that way. He appears to be totally satisfied with temporal things and yet always needs more "stuff" to keep him happy. He is very much a creature of this world. I think about Nabal. As I read about loving the fool and coming to a place of repentance concerning my own attitudes, I question if it is even possible to have a meeting of minds with the fool. Then I remember, I can't make it happen, it is God who does the real work. I just have to be willing and available. Is there disappointment? Yes, of course. But God says to be of good courage because He will go with us wherever we go and will be faithful to see us through into the future. God is faithful, human beings are not. *I'm* not faithful.

In fact, as I viewed Abigail I realized how much I had to grow up. I always considered myself as stable and level headed. It shocked me to realize how emotionally *sick* I had been all this time! I wanted to throw myself on the floor and kick and scream in frustration.

I determined to re-establish my life with God and grow up. I would always be hostage to emotional reactions and behaviors unless I really meant to seek God's face and His will in my life. Did I really want freedom? Did I really want to know where God would lead me? How could I believe Him unless I knew Him well? How could I know Him unless I spent time with Him? How could I trust that He would make good on His promises unless I knew Him?

I resolved to pray and spend time reading the Bible regularly and to expect that God would answer by reforming my heart and my thinking.

I went about learning, as Apostle Paul said, to be content in being abased or abounding in every circumstance and situation before I could make any life changing decisions. If my mind was on God's protection and plans for me, then I could persevere through anything that came my way. Even if the future looked unfathomable. This meant sticking to good resolutions or judgments to move forward no matter what I saw or felt.

Henry G. Bosch, in *Our Daily Bread* said,

"A weak faith may appear to be strong when friends are true, the body is healthy, and the business is profitable. But a truly strong faith clings to the Lord's promises and relies on His faithfulness when loved ones leave, health departs and dark clouds obscure the future.

Evangelist D. L. Moody once said, 'Trust in yourself and you are doomed to disappointment; trust in your friends and they will die and leave you; but trust in God and you will never be confounded in time or eternity. Don't murmur and rebel in your hour of adversity. Learn to trust God in every trial.'"[8]

I had to work through much twisted thinking. I reminded myself that God can do anything. I didn't understand that He works around our free wills to bring about His purposes in our lives. Still, little by little I was learning to get out of the way of protecting and cushioning Dean to allow God to do whatever He was going to do in any given situation.

God once gave me a picture for Dean. A huge tree stood by a river. Its trunk was great and strong. The overloaded limbs were bowing nearly to the ground and it was alive with birdsong. I was impressed that the interpretation meant that Dean would be like a strong tree, a father of many. He had missed that as a child, but God is in the business of redemption. I wanted the promise in that long ago picture fulfilled so much—for him, for us as a family, and for others "out there." Over and over I begged, prayed, "stood in proxy" for him at church, tried to control every crisis situation so he would have to "shape up" and all to no avail.

When God asked me what I wanted—that was it.

Yet God pursued further. What did I want for myself? That was a new thought. God wanted to know what I wanted for *myself*? Wasn't I just an extension of Dean?

Wow! I wanted to know what it would mean to be whole and holy before God and to be with God. I wanted a healthy identity in the Christ who saved me. I wanted to see God as best I could while still living in this fleshly body. I didn't want to be looking around Dean's shoulder at God. I wanted to be free to be whoever God was calling *me* to be and free to do whatever God was calling *me* to do.

And I wanted to be free to be happy regardless of circumstances, because I was trusting, really and truly trusting, in the goodness of my God to handle everything set before me.

The Bridge

As I persevered through a new way of thinking, I have come to believe that perseverance and letting go can be, as the cliché says, "Two sides of the same coin." As I persevered through growing towards freedom of spirit and health, I could see that letting go would be one of the most important tools.

One of those points in Pastor Steve's sermon had to do with letting go. He said, "Sometimes a new beginning requires the end of an old way."[9]

Melody Beattie wrote a daily meditation book called *The Language of Letting Go*. On February 12th she talked about a bridge in a section called "Letting Go of Those Not In Recovery."

I love the imagery she portrayed here. It was something I could really move forward through. I practiced this over and over.

She wrote:

We can go forward with our life and recoveries, even though someone we love is not yet recovering. Picture a bridge. On one side of the bridge it is cold and dark. We stood there with others in the cold and darkness, doubled over in pain … we did not know there was a bridge. We thought we were trapped on a cliff.[10]

Hmmm … it seems I remembered something about that cliff. She went on:

Our eyes opened, by the Grace of God, because it was time. We saw the bridge. People told us what was on the other side: warmth, light and healing from our pain. We could barely glimpse or imagine this, but we decided to start the trek across the bridge anyway.

We tried to convince the people around us on the cliff that there was a bridge to a better place, but they wouldn't listen. They couldn't see it; they couldn't believe. They were not ready for the journey.[11]

I had tried to convince Dean to walk across the bridge with me. He would not. He kept saying life was hopeless. It could not be different. He could not see the grace of God. Melody continued:

We decided to go alone, because we believed, and because people on the other side were cheering us onward. The closer we got to the other side, the more we could see, and feel, that what we had been promised was real. There was light, warmth, healing and love. The other side was a better place.

But now, there is a bridge between us and those on the other side. Sometimes, we may be tempted to go back and drag them over with us, but it cannot be done. No one can be dragged or forced across this bridge. Each person must go at his or her own choice, when the time is right. Some will come; some will stay on the other side. The choice is not ours.[12]

Oh my, what a hard lesson to learn. To go across the bridge and leave the loved ones behind who refuse to cross. Such a great struggle ensues when it is time to cross the bridge—alone. Especially when the circumstances don't change, yet you are now on the other side of the bridge. This is where it costs to persevere! Melody said:

> We can love them. We can wave to them. We can holler back and forth. We can cheer them on, as others have cheered and encouraged us. But we cannot make them come over with us.
>
> If our time has come to cross the bridge, or if we have already crossed and are standing in the light and warmth, we do not have to feel guilty. It is where we are meant to be. We do not have to go back to the dark cliff because another's time has not yet come.[13]

Why is it that we need permission to do what is best for all concerned? Cross the bridge … accept God's healing and warmth … don't feel guilty … love and wave to those who haven't come, but stay in the light. It's what we want to do. It's the best thing to do. So, let's go do it. God is calling us.

New Name

Sometime as I was crossing that bridge, I remembered listening to Chuck Swindoll asking on his broadcast, *Insight For Living*, "What is your name? If you were to be given a spiritual name by others, what would it be? What single sentence would be your epitaph?"

Glibly I answered aloud, "Contentious. Here lies a contentious woman."

God's protest immediately boomed through my mind. *Stop the tape!* He was angry. *You have no business answering like that. Am I not the God who sent my Son to die and resurrect in order to save you from just that? You once were that contentious woman, but I have formed conditions and circumstances to change you. If you insist on continuing to call yourself that which you once were but are not now due to rebirth, which cost my*

Son His life, then my wrath is kindled against you. I have fashioned a new life and a new name for you.

Phew! I dropped to my knees. Yes, I know He was giving me a new name, and often I have failed to act out that new name. Yet as I seek Him, He will be found. He is there all the time just waiting.

Am I not the same Shepherd that will follow that one lost lamb?

That would be me. I am to cast my care on Him and He will care for me. I am to relax and let Him carry those burdens that I cannot carry.

The true answers to those questions?

Name: Endurance

Epitaph: She endured to the end.

Come Away

Larry Crabb said in *Finding God*, "Future hope is more valuable than present relief. Until we realize this, we are not on the path to finding God."[14]

God says to seek Him, turn our hearts to Him and He will be found. If we do our "duty" and do it without Him in it, all we will see are flames as it burns up in the end. Only those things done in Him will remain. If we feel loneliness, then we must seek Him. It seems He must get our attention by letting us go in our busy lives until we get ourselves into places of desperation then we grow thirsty and seek His company. We can do nothing without Him.

We need to seek our God in quietness. He is saying, *Come away, My beloved,* but we are too busy. He has to arrange our circumstances so that we regret not seeking Him. He wants us to search Him out and not our own pleasures or let the cares of the world wrap us up too tightly.

I realized I wanted that future hope much more than the present relief. I wanted to find God.

Only then could He restore the fruits of the Spirit and relationship to me.

> *Come away, My beloved.*
> He is calling and sweeping aside all other issues.
> *Come away, My beloved.*
> He said He would keep His promises to me and to my children.
> *Come away, My beloved.*
> He said joy would come after weeping.
> *Come away, My beloved.*
> He said I would see His goodness.
> *Come away, My beloved.*
> His love is burning.
> *Come away, My beloved.*
> Do you hear Him?

Chapter Seven

Wrestling With Death

Learning About God's Watchful Care

I will lift up my eyes to the hills—from whence comes my help?
My help comes from the Lord, Who made heaven and earth.
(Ps. 121:1, 2)

Arms of God

I walked into the house a little after 11 PM on Friday. The weekend. The youth event I had just headed up for the evening was over and I longed for my bed. On the way home I wondered, as usual, what I was going to find.

I put my purse and papers down on the table upon coming in. "It's quiet," I murmured, "Well, it's late on a Friday night. Why shouldn't it be quiet? He should be in bed by now. Guess I should check on him."

I started down the stairs to the basement and stopped. His feet came into view. Still on the floor. Still in the very same position as they were five hours ago when I left him sleeping, or was it passed out? Five hours ago I thought he was safe to be left alone. He couldn't hurt himself. I sank down on the step.

The cats across the room were curled up and watchful.

"No, Lord, it can't be! Not what I've always feared." I sat there on the step for a moment, trying to keep calm, telling myself not to jump to conclusions here. He was so still. I couldn't see his chest moving. His skin looked … ! "No! God! It can't be!"

I gulped for breath as I ran down the stairs and dropped next to Dean. I hesitated before touching him. No pulse. Cooling skin. The screaming in my head became audible. This was the most frightening thing I had ever encountered! What do I do?

WHAT DO I DO?

I'm here, Child. I will not leave you alone.

Call 911—that was it.

I sensed Daddy God's arms around me and felt His presence in that valley of death.

"Calm down, Ma'am. Tell us what happened…"

What happened? How should I know? Was it drugs? Alcohol? A bookcase lay on the floor. It looked like he'd been working on it and maybe bumped his head as he fell from it or did it fall from him? Had he passed out standing up?

"We'll get someone there as quickly as we can …"

Nearly an hour later, the paramedics, the police, the coroner all showed up. I waited at the door for them. I didn't even want to be in the house. Still, I felt the arms of God around me, just the comfort of knowing He was with me helped me to wait calmly. Two friends came and stayed with me all night as the officials did their duty.

At four in the morning, they brought him up in a bag. "I can't see this," I said. My companions, Jennene and Vivian, and I moved to a bedroom and shut the door until it was over.

"Ma'am, here are the numbers in case you need anything … " this piece of paper closed a very long chapter of my life.

"You're coming home with me," Jennene, insisted. The face of the clock showed nearly five in the morning. I was so grateful. I knew I could not stay in the house alone in what was left of the February night.

She took me home and led me to a bedroom. The light stayed on. I couldn't bring myself to plunge the room into darkness. There had been so much of it. I had to have the light. Somehow the knowledge that death could happen at any time over the years does not make the reality any easier. Stunned, unbelieving, amazed, unreal, none of those words can call forth the truth of reality.

I stared at the wall. Suddenly a picture appeared. I heard Jesus say in my mind, *don't worry about him anymore, he is with me now.* I saw Dean walking across a golden bridge spanning a river. I somehow knew it was the River of Life. The streets of gold were before him, and the crystal palaces reflected beautiful rainbow colors. The light was incredible. I didn't know grass could be so green. A tree stood beside the river, but I could not figure out from which side of the river it grew. Suddenly I realized that Jesus was walking alongside Dean with his arm around Dean's shoulders. The picture disappeared.

I immediately grabbed my Bible and turned to Revelation 21 and 22. Yes, there it was—the City of God. I saw it! *I saw it!* I did not know until I saw it that the Tree of Life grows on *both* sides of the river! I saw it and then I read it! What an incredible gift God had given me.

"Therefore, my beloved brethren, be steadfast, immovable, always abounding in the work of the Lord, knowing that your labor is not in vain in the Lord" (1 Cor. 15:58).

God just gave me that assurance that my labor was not in vain. Even through such strange and surreal events, I knew that Dean was happy and whole for the first time in his life. If any of us could see him now, he would be a different Dean than ever we have known before. I would never wish him back here to the tragic suffering he lived through on earth.

I believe Father God had mercy on him and said, *Ok, son, this is enough. It's time for you to come home.* Dean is comforted now; there is no more pain, no more sorrow, and Jesus has wiped away all his tears.

I learned something else that night. Our Father God is excited about our homecoming. He can't wait to show us what He has been preparing for us. Scripture says that precious in God's eyes is the death of His saints. Why? I discovered that He can hardly contain the anticipation of the day He calls us home. He has so much to share with us and *HE LOVES US* with an everlasting love.

What comfort in dark days!

Tomatoes?

The days that followed were much like most funerals. Dearly loved ones brought food and comfort. My children and I planned the funeral in one accord. Amazing. Only one thing presented a problem for us, the flowers.

We looked and looked over the pictures of flower sprays. Finally, my son, Jeff, said, "Why don't we just put tomato plants on the casket?" Daughter Angela and I looked at each other in astonishment.

"I'm kidding! I'm kidding!"

"We're not!"

Dean loved to grow tomato plants. He had growing contests with his friends, Roger and Don. I think he won sometimes, though Roger or Don might contest that.

Tomatoes on his casket would be perfect. But it was February. The funeral director found a florist who would mix silk plants with hot house tomatoes and roses. It was beautiful. Dean would have loved it. I noticed the deer certainly loved it, too, a couple days later when I visited his grave. I think that would have pleased him.

Our final goodbye to him was a family group hug next to the casket.

Was It Worth It?

Following Dean's death, the peace and quiet in the house was both shocking and calm at first. I could not quite relax. A lifetime of being on guard, day and night, took its toll. Reality began to set in along with the mountains of paperwork and legal demands.

As I wandered through the house, memories alternately soothed, made me laugh, or attacked me. I remembered when, as a brand new Christian, I asked God to make my life a living sacrifice unto him. I grinned and shook my head as I reviewed what that "living sacrifice" entailed. If I had known the outcome, would I have ever asked this of God? I'm sure I would not. No one chooses such a road.

Up till now, my purpose seemed to be to bring one lost sheep back to the Shepherd. As I considered the picture of Dean walking into heaven, I sensed Jesus asking me, *was it worth it?*

What a question. How does one answer such a question?

Of course, it was worth seeing Dean walk into heaven. It was worth seeing Jesus' arm around Dean's shoulders. It was worth the small glimpse of heaven I was privileged to see. It was very much worth knowing that heaven is a real place, just as the Bible describes it, and that Jesus invites us to come and even ushers us in. Yes, it was worth it.

What is thirty years of suffering in this life compared to someone's eternity?

What is that? Back up. Thirty years of suffering? How long is our life expectancy on this earth? Last I heard it is about seventy years or so. Thirty, out of seventy years, is a lot of time. How could God ask that of me? I came back to considering that "reasonable service" again. And does God *really* mean it?

It seems he does.

I answered "yes." I didn't do the enduring thing very perfectly. It happened one day at a time, sometimes even one hour at a time as endurance was given. I did my share of kicking and screaming. Yet because of God's constant grace and presence, I did endure to the end. "If we endure, we shall also reign with Him" (2 Tim. 2:12).

We may not always endure with a cheerful face, but it is our heart that God calls to endurance. Will we allow Him the free reign to complete His design in us on earth as He completes it in heaven?

Reigning with Him in heaven will be forever. Enduring here on earth may be only thirty or seventy years. Is it worth it? Consider!

He Never Sleeps Nor Slumbers

"He will not allow your foot to be moved; He who keeps you will not slumber. Behold, He who keeps Israel shall neither slumber nor sleep" (Ps. 121:3, 4).

For a while it felt like death was everywhere. It is the last great enemy to life on earth. The unconquerable. I've always thought of death as the door to eternity and how wonderful it will be to see Jesus and be with Him forever. So it will—when the time comes. But for now I was not prepared for the starkness of death. The door looked frightful even though I knew it would be only for a moment; because once we leave the body, we are present with the Lord. The starkness and horror is on earth for those of us left behind to work through. We all must go that way.

"The Lord is your keeper; The Lord is your shade at your right hand. The sun shall not strike you by day, Nor the moon by night" (Ps. 121:5, 6).

I clung to this psalm day and night for months. I wrestled with what I believed about spiritual things and how to live a practical daily life. A new dimension to living entered in, and for the first time I had to acknowledge that this life truly *is* fragile. I kept wondering if I would be next. How grateful I was for a God that never slept or relaxed His guard over me, day or night.

I learned that nightmares are a normal part of the aftermath of the death of a family member. I did not expect this. I relived the tragedy of the old life over and over in my unconscious mind and woke up in the middle of the night screaming and afraid.

A sense of despair weighed heavily after waking from one of those dreams. I put a light on and finally shook off the cloak of night-time unreality and picked up my Bible. I asked my Father to help me, and I heard Him say in my mind, *My arms are open wide. Come, Child.* I was finally able to turn out the light again, in peace, knowing I was in my Father's protective arms.

Another time, it was me dying. I knew my destination when my life on earth ended. Jesus died on the cross that I might have eternal life. I knew it. So it surprised me to be afraid after all. Even after that wonderful assurance that Jesus let me see the night Dean went home to be with Him. I knew that Jesus would be waiting for me with His arms stretched out wide. There is no fear in that knowledge.

Yet the bleakness of death is scary. Pictures of being trapped in an evil box in the ground and being unable to escape troubled me. Maybe I saw too many scary movies as a child. I knew that the body was non-functional without the God-breathed life of the soul and spirit, and that part will be in the City of God with Jesus and will never see the gloom of the grave.

Still, at two or three o'clock in the morning, it's pretty dark. This must be why the Bible as the Word of God is a lamp to our feet and a light to our paths.

Sharing the Burden of Pain

I struggled to believe God. Who of us doesn't during such times? Even when we know that we know He is our Father and He is good. But our emotions want to tell us otherwise.

I know God told me through the Bible that He would provide a future and a hope for me. He had work for me to do, and through a psalm, I understood His promise of a lifetime yet in which to serve Him. With such promises given through the Scriptures, how could I doubt Him? I didn't want to doubt. My God was faithful. My feelings were not.

I'm always surprised at how, when we ask Him, God brings to us help. It may be people, circumstances, or, in my case in this season, a book. A friend advised me to read Jerry Sittser's book, *A Grace Disguised.* I think I underlined most of it. The author had lost several beloved family members at the same time and God took him through some deep, cold waters.

As I read his book, I was comforted to know that somebody understood. At one point he said that his loss would be with him forever but the passage of time mitigated it somewhat. He wrote about feelings of pain, panic, and chaos. I thought about how I had spent a lifetime becoming quite familiar with those feelings. I still felt more panic and chaos than pain, although I remembered the extremities of pain throughout the years.

I didn't realize until I read Jerry Sittser's book, how much of Dean's pain I had carried along with my own. My anger at him had overshadowed nearly everything else. Yet underlying that anger was shared pain. Reading through Jerry's book held a mirror up to my face and I saw that pain and recognized it. On my knees, I released it. I could not believe the relief as that heavy burden lifted from me.

Now I am grateful because, for Dean, heaven has dropped away those burdensome chains forever. I am grateful for me because I don't have to face those unknown terrors on earth anymore.

Jerry says his soul was stretched.[1] What a good way to put it. It's so strange how grief, fun, sorrow, and joy can all happen at the same time. Yes, pain and pleasure, tragedy and crisis, life and death—sometimes *all at the same time*. What a journey!

For a time I still had trouble believing good things could be ahead. I was too conditioned to expect disaster and crisis. But God is *always* for our good. It doesn't matter what the package looks like. He is about our good.

We put a psalm on Dean's headstone. It was always true, for Dean and for all of God's children. It is still true.

"The Lord will command His loving kindness in the daytime, And in the night His song shall be with me—A prayer to the God of my life" (Ps. 42:8).

Misunderstood Grief

One of the most famous Bible stories is that of David and Bathsheba.[2] David, the King of Israel, stayed home while his armies were away engaging in battle with the enemy. David didn't realize that the enemy of his soul stayed home with him.

So the story goes—he saw the beautiful wife of one of his valiant men. He lusted after her and while her husband was putting his life on the line for love of God, country, and king, the king was busy committing adultery with this valiant man's wife.

Bathsheba became pregnant and told David. David immediately set about finding a solution to his problem. First David called Uriah, Bathsheba's husband, home during the battle. Maybe the baby could be passed off as Uriah's. Good plan! Only David didn't count on

Uriah's integrity. A warrior kept himself set apart while his comrades were in battle. Uriah did not sleep with his wife, Bathsheba.

This thwarted King David's Plan A. He decided the next best thing to do would be to put Uriah, the warrior husband, in harm's way and hope for his death. Plan B worked.

David brought Uriah's grieving widow into his household. Did this cover it up and make it all better? Well … no. Nathan the Prophet came and revealed the truth. David repented of his sin, but Nathan declared the child would die.

The time came when the child was born and he was very ill. Scripture says, "David therefore pleaded with God for the child, and David fasted and went in and lay all night on the ground" (2 Sam. 12:16).

I think anyone with a deeply ill loved one, especially a child, can relate to pleading, fasting, and laying on your face before God. Tears flow and every sobbing breath squeezes the heart. Is there ever a time when you feel so helpless?

Even when others come with food or drink—it is just too impossible to consider eating or drinking when a chasm of life and death is before you.

Then the unthinkable happens. The loved one dies.

David's advisors were afraid to tell him because his reaction to his child's death could be so terrifying when they considered his grief as the child lay ill. But he heard them whispering among themselves.

"Is the child dead?" And they said, "He is dead."

"So David arose from the ground, washed and anointed himself, and changed his clothes; and he went into the house of the Lord and worshiped. Then he went to his own house; and when he requested, they set food before him, and he ate" (2 Sam. 12:19, 20).

What? He had just heard that his child, for whom he deeply grieved, had died. Now he cleaned himself up, worshipped God, and ate breakfast like nothing happened? What's going on?

David answered them, "While the child was still alive, I fasted and wept; for I said, 'Who can tell whether the Lord will be gracious to me, that the child may live?' But now he is dead; why should I fast? Can I bring him back again? I shall go to him, but he shall not return to me" (2 Sam. 12:22, 23).

What a very powerful statement David made!

I pondered this statement for a long time. After Dean passed away I received a lot of sympathy. That was as it should be. Most people who lose spouses are devastated. It is not just a matter of losing a loved one. Your identity changes, your lifestyle changes, your place in society changes, just about everything changes. This is a time that the old "fish out of water" feeling is the truth. You just don't fit into any of the familiar places.

Something else was disturbing me. The relief and the freedom I was experiencing made me feel like a fraud. I thought I was supposed to be crying and hiding away and depressed. Instead, I thought unlimited possibilities were now opening before me. I thought I had to hide the relief and my optimistic outlook because I was a new widow. I was expected to grieve. How unnatural of me to feel such joy!

I sought some help for my discomfort. I joined a group to work through the grief. The group therapist asked me if I had given myself permission to grieve deeply. That required thought.

Those times in my "scrub tree" car where I screamed and cried out at God in the dark—before I believed that He saw me—could that be grief? The times spent in prayer and tears beside Dean's chair when he might have died, but didn't—could that be grief? What about the times when I had to get him to bed because of drugs, alcohol, or what I thought of as "out of mind" experiences—was that grief? Each time I came home from work and had to sit in my car and pray for courage to go inside the house to face whoever he was that day—was that grief?

I wondered if I shouldn't grieve so much.

As I looked further into this grief thing, I remembered how much grieving I did through the years when Dean was alive. I don't miss that life. It was stressful and often terrifying. I grieved over the desperation that we lived daily and the fear of death constantly stalking until the phantom became the reality. I grieved that it turned out the way it did.

I grieved for all that was missed.

I remember shortly after Dean passed away another man died and left a widow. It seemed to myself and others, that I should be able to comfort her because this was still a new way of life for me. Only, I could not help her. I could not relate to the devastating grief she was experiencing. That lack bothered me and I thought something was wrong with me.

After much prayer and examination, it finally occurred to me that it was ok to be happy and looking ahead and relieved after Dean left this earth. Like David, I had been on my face before God with tears and anguish, fasting and praying, crying out in grief—*for years through the trials as they happened.* Then, when Dean passed away, I got up, washed myself, worshipped God, and ate breakfast. *And it was ok!*

Preserved In Coming and Going

"The Lord shall preserve you from all evil; He shall preserve your soul. The Lord shall preserve your going out and your coming in from this time forth, and even forevermore" (Ps. 121:7, 8).

"May 29: Today was our wedding anniversary. I came to the cemetery and brought some flowers and a flag with me. The bright sun is pleasantly warm, except when a breeze gusts. I am sitting on Dean's grave and looking about at the flowers announcing Memorial Day all over the cemetery," I mused in my journal.

"I see a young man a few graves away doing the same as me. I guess that he is grieving for a young wife who is gone before her time. Poor man. I don't know quite what I am doing here. Dean is not here. He is in heaven. I am just sitting here and enjoying the peace.

"I remember the wedding that happened all those years ago today. How very different we were then and how life did not turn out anything like what we'd hoped and dreamed."

Don't look back, Child; it is passed away. I AM doing a new thing; there will be a road in the wilderness and rivers in the desert. I have a future for you.

"Sometimes I feel like a swinging pendulum. I've heard people talking about this. Side to side, I am unable to point myself in a direction and go that way. It's so frustrating."

One day at a time. I know the plans I have for you. But they are not yet. I want you to wait for now.

"Waiting … waiting … "

Our Father God is so gentle with us when we are drifting through pain. We think we have to do something, but He wants to sit quietly with us and let our souls soak up the sunshine of His love. He preserves our going and our coming.

This is truly a gift. Will we recognize it?

Growing Our Souls

One night as my Small Group was doing a study in James, Chuck Swindoll said the word for "various" meant something like "polka-dot." He fleshed that out by saying that trials come in all shapes, colors, and sizes. Trials are designed by God. Chuck said they are inevitable and have purpose. They are to test our faith to make it enduring, and he called trials "servants for character development." He reminded us that David, in the Psalms, cries that God will deliver us out of them all. Finally, he said, "wisdom is having God's insight to understand the test. Faith is having God's strength to endure the test."[3]

Wow! I thought about how God had been developing character in me. It's a good thing I've always liked variety, because trials have certainly been "polka-dot" in my life. I've had such "shapes, colors, and sizes" that the kaleidoscope sends me spinning.

I think we all wonder at times what God can be working out in us. Why must there be such a variety of trials? How far do the depths of our souls go? And we wonder how far will God go with us?

Philippians 3 talks about forgetting what is passed and reaching toward what is ahead, pressing on to the goal.[4] What could be that goal? Actually two goals come to mind. The first would be to know Jesus as intimately as possible, and the second is to be like Him. We come around again to that living sacrifice that Jesus modeled.

In order to know Jesus, to be like Him, and to do what He did, we must trust Him. In Ephesians it says that if we can place ourselves before Him, Father God will strengthen us with the might of His Spirit. He will see to it that Jesus will dwell in our hearts through faith. Then, because we are rooted and grounded in His love, which we might not recognize without pain, we can understand the width, length, depth, and the height of His love for us.[5]

After this understanding, we can be filled with the fullness of God and we can trust Him to do more than we can imagine. Even *exceedingly abundantly* more than we can dream. His power is given to us, His children, and through the working of that power, through the pain it takes to grow our souls, He is glorified.

Jerry Sittser says, "God will continue to be present to the end of my life and through all eternity. God is *growing my soul*, making it bigger, and filling it with Himself. My life is being transformed. Though I have endured pain, I believe that the outcome is going to be wonderful."[6]

I have to agree with Jerry. God is with me and always will be. He reminds me of His presence constantly. My life will never be the same as new adventures invite me. I can hardly wait for God's plan to unfold. Yes, I have endured pain, but I could not know just how wonderful God could be, or life could be, without the pain.

My response to Jerry's, "What matters is the movement forward"[7] is amen and amen.

CHAPTER EIGHT

TRUST AND ASSURANCE

Trusting in God's Promise to be Present

Oil of joy for mourning … The planting of the Lord, that He may be glorified. (Isa. 61:3)

Diagnosis: Cancer

Cancer surprised me. I suppose everybody, like me, thinks it can't happen to them. Only it does.

The first time breast cancer invaded my body, the week flew by in a whirlwind. Monday we did a biopsy. Tuesday my husband and I met the doctor at his office and got the news. Wednesday I lost a breast. Thursday I went home with my drains (left over from surgery), and Friday I got the lab results—all clear. What a relief! My doctor went on vacation and I met his partner for follow up.

Life changed. Since the process happened so fast, there had been no opportunity to explore reconstruction alternatives. I found out that reconstruction for a breast cancer survivor meets more than just a need for vanity.

Over the next few years I hated trying on new clothes. One side fit and the other hung lopsided. I tried several kinds of prosthetics and they all fit differently. What really upset me, though, were swimming parties. Few swimsuits had pockets and they had to be sewn in. Once I got to the beach, a decision had to be made concerning diving into the lake and risk losing the costly prosthesis. How does water reach in and grab it? I still haven't figured that out. If I left the prosthesis on the beach (under cover, of course) and swam without it, another problem presented itself. One side of my suit, weighted with water, dropped to my belly button as I exited the lake. This was not cool, only drafty.

For several years I suffered through this situation of having one breast but the time was not wasted. I did my homework and learned about reconstruction options. I figured, over time, given the same body with the same conditions, my chances of cancer recurrence were pretty good.

I would be ready for it the next time.

Jars of Oil

In the Old Testament, 2 Kings tells the story of a widow urgently seeking out Elisha, the prophet of God.[1]

"Elisha, my husband is dead. You know he was a godly man. Now the creditors are coming to take my children as slaves in payment." I can only imagine her panic. *God, do something!*

Although Elisha could be testy, he immediately reacted in gentleness to help her.

"What do you want me to do? What do you have in your house that we can work with?"

"I only have a jar of oil in the house," she cried in despair.

"All right, then. Borrow jars and jugs from every place you can find them—from your house, from your neighbors, lying around the roadways—any place you can find them. Make sure they are empty and get as many as you can. Don't limit them as long as you can find them."

"Once you have lined them up in your house, close your doors behind you and your sons. Begin filling up the containers with your jar of oil. As soon as one is filled, have a son grab another and fill it until they are all full."

Elisha walked away and the widow wasted no time in following his instructions. I don't know what kind of deadline she labored under, but it's clear that she was in a hurry to collect those containers and fill them.

She asked no questions of Elisha. I might have said something like, "What! Are you crazy? What are you talking about oil for when I need money to pay creditors? Don't you get it? They are going to take my boys away!"

No, this widow just set about following instructions. Fast.

After collecting jars and filling ... and filling ... and filling, the time came when she asked for another jug and one of her sons said, "Mom, there are no more containers. They are all full."

The oil stopped flowing.

The widow went out of her house to find Elisha and reported that the jars were full and the oil stopped.

He must have smiled kindly at her as he said, "Go then, sell the oil and pay the debt. After your affairs are settled, you and your sons will have enough left over to live on."

I don't know what her reaction was, but I would think she must have dropped to the ground and kissed his face as her tears poured.

A desperate mother has desperate reactions. Her faithfulness was rewarded. I think God must have been very pleased with her.

So what does this story have to do with cancer?

The truth is that God will supply our every need as we come to him in faith.

When we get a diagnosis of cancer or some other illness that is either life threatening or life changing, our natural reaction is to panic. I'm sure most of us cry out, "God, do something! Hurry!" Truly fear, panic, and mourning come much more naturally to us because we live in a fallen world that is trained to see darkness.

The ruler of this world—our debtor—is coming. He brings sorrow, suffering, and death. It takes a lot of equipping to face cancer or other kinds of debilitating diseases. Some diseases are more survivable than others, but life will not be the same ever again in either case. He is busy battering our souls through our fragile bodies. God says in the Scriptures that He holds our tears in bottles in heaven. A song describes an alabaster box. I am so glad that He is closely concerned with us in the harm we endure on earth.

The oil that comes from God, pouring out joy, blessings, healing, anointing, and many other wonders, streams as long as our faith can contain it. The woman in the story had to search for every jar she could find, far and wide, and God kept the oil rushing for her until the last one was filled. Then the oil spigot stopped.

During times of extended anguish, we have need of courage, humor, wisdom, adaptability, tenacity, rest, pleasure, faith, joy, community support, and many other things. I think of each one as a jar that I bring to God to fill. We can't make these things happen in our souls; in fact, the Scriptures say that it is not even our responsibility to conjure up something from an empty soul. God expects us to exercise our faith to bring each empty jar to Him as it is needed, and He provides the activating agent: Holy Spirit oil.

We can choose to trust God and let Him fill each jar through each circumstance that comes to us. As long as our faith provides the jar, God will fill it with redemption. When we have no more faith, there is no more oil.

Sometimes we may have to go out and search for another faith jar because we just don't have one that fits the situation. This is where community comes in. Loved ones, family, and friends, can help find jars for us. If we will allow them to do so, they will wrap us in their love as they pray, send notes of encouragement, do practical acts of service for us, or attend to whatever the needs are.

Sometimes our jars can look pretty ridiculous. Others may even question us, saying things like, "do you know what you are doing?" or "why are you going this way? Common sense says to go that way" or "if you don't follow this path, then dire consequences may follow." When we act on a nudge from God, our obedience may look strange to others. I'm sure the hurry in which the woman in the story sought out her jars looked pretty strange to her neighbors. How can we know what God will do for us unless we step out in ridiculous faith? He still does miracles regardless of how they may look at the outset. We can't limit Him or we may find that we will receive nothing from Him.

As we hold out our jars of faith and ready ourselves for His answers, whatever they are, God fills us with His anointing oil. We are made to reveal His glory in us.

The Other Shoe Falls

"They didn't like my 'mams' again and I have to do them over. They are talking ultrasound. Biopsy is the next stage and then surgery. I am at stage two now in this cancer journey. Again," I mused after receiving a phone call one evening after work. This phone call came as a result of a mammogram examination.

I'd been down this road before. Breast cancer doesn't always happen again, but I have seen it repeated often enough. Just the week before

I told Cherrie, my nurse practitioner, that if this is the year that the "other shoe is to fall," then I would insist it be a double reconstruction. She agreed that it was a good plan.

For years, cancer walked beside me. I had once been cured of breast cancer, yet I somehow felt it was not over. Every year if I got a clean bill of health, I breathed a sigh of relief. "Not this year," I'd think. "Safe for a while."

Now it seemed this was the year. Maybe God was restoring the years the locusts had eaten in this area for me. Maybe this year God would allow a complete healing and a restored body. For so long I could not even think about it. To me other matters were more important. I just hoped I would not have to do chemo or radiation this time.

This is where the rubber would really meet the road. This is where I would find out if I truly surrendered my life, my body, and my everything to Jesus. Even if it meant bad news. Yikes! My eyes would need to be trained to look beyond this unimaginable road to lock onto the good news of heaven.

If my time on earth was coming to a close, then I would think of shutting my eyes to earth to see Jesus' smiling face and His hands held out to me. Then we walk hand in hand across the golden bridge to the City of God. Forever together! God is good. All the time. No matter what.

A Partner in Cancer

The sun had disappeared and the evening had come. City lights winked as far as the eye could see from the hospital waiting room in the surgical wing. My dear friend, Carolyn, was in recovery. She'd had a mastectomy that afternoon, every woman's bad dream.

Several of us waited, some of us since early afternoon. Others, like me, had come after work. It seemed like such a long time. We were wondering if Carolyn was all right or if they found something worse than expected.

"I'm going to go see," said Arlie. She went right into the recovery room of the day surgery to see how Carolyn's recovery was coming along. I didn't know she could do that!

Arlie came out a little shaken, but Carolyn was fine. "She looks so white under all those bandages and sheets, but they said she's coming out of the anesthetic just fine and surgery went well."

It wasn't long before a parade of us followed Carolyn's orderlies as they wheeled her from the recovery wing to her room since she would be spending the night after all. She did alternate moaning and smiling as she heard our hushed conversation as we marched along beside her.

It's Official

As a follow up to the phone call, when I received the official papers in the mail requesting my repeat performance with the mammo-smasher, I thought it interesting that the technician had said the reports had been clear before I left the clinic. However, these papers said, "the results of your exam indicate the need for additional evaluation." Hmm. If they were clear, there should not be further need of evaluation, unless a problem existed.

Well, back to good news/bad news. Which would it be? I was not afraid of the dying part, but I *was* afraid of the chemotherapy or radiation. Journeys of friends were fresh in my mind. Still if it went like the last time I had this problem, it would be contained in the breast and I would get that double reconstruction and it would be all over and for good! No more wondering about results every spring.

I knew by now that I could not really live until I was ready to die. I faced my own death after Dean died and fought with those demons then. I came out of that battle knowing whom I have believed!

It's only when that battle has been fought that it can be possible to truly live and to be ready to give all you are and all you have in service to the one who holds your life in His hands. His requirements may mean that you give up your life for another either by living or by dying. After what He has given up for us, how can we do less?

When I thought of some of my loved ones, I wondered if I would be willing to give up my life if only they would believe. I know exactly where I am going and who is taking me there. They do not.

All these thoughts ran through my mind as I pondered the next round of testing. If it was cancer, I wanted the show on the road. I had too many plans to wait around. I wanted to be recovering as soon as possible. Not to mention getting "It" before it might be too late. God willing.

Coffee and Cancer

I wouldn't wish illness on anybody, but it sure was nice to have my friend, Carolyn, in the fight with me. I'd always been alone before. Now we could encourage one another along this dubious path.

"I remember trying to open my eyes as they wheeled me along because I could hear all of you," Carolyn was saying one morning as we stopped for lattes after a doctor visit. "I couldn't help smiling."

"Yeah and it took them so long to get you settled that we all went to the cafeteria for dinner. We were so grateful that you came through with flying colors." I stirred my coffee before taking another sip.

"I had so much love flowing toward me. It was awesome. You gals came alongside and loved me through it."

I had to know. "How are you dealing with the results?"

She paused thoughtfully. "After surgery I didn't want to look. It's like you go from being a woman to a thing. It took a while to get used to what happened. I don't want to wait to do reconstruction."

The next time we were together, it was my turn. The results from the repeat tests showed calcifications. Déjà vu! Those things were cancerous last time we did this. Immediately after the tests I went home and made appointments with surgeons. Somehow I was able to get appointments with both doctors within days. I wasn't waiting for anything.

It looked like the hand of God to me. He sent Carolyn and me to each other at this time. We went together to doctors and biopsies, and did our reconstruction research together. It was wonderful to have a friend and not go it alone. God cared for both of us.

In the first days of spring that year, it snowed six inches. What a great time to experience a biopsy for cancer. More winter when it was supposed to be spring. Carolyn went with me to my biopsy. The doctor let her watch and in spite of all that she had been through herself, she nearly passed out. I wanted to laugh but my position at the time was rather painful. We had a good time together over lunch after that and the next wait for results had begun.

I will walk through this with you, Daughter. You will not be alone. I created those empty spaces in your heart and I will fill them. For now—give them to Me. Haven't I promised delight?

First, this road to wholeness must be traveled, and I will never leave you nor forsake you. Trust Me. I Am for you. Wait, Daughter, I have great things in store for you. Wait on Me. Walk this road patiently and confidently. It is for your best. For I love you and desire good things for you. You are a delight to My heart.

Life is an adventure. Our Lord has things in store for us that we don't know about. But we know that He does, and He is completely trustworthy.

"I had to think about dying, too, and I wasn't planning on thinking about that right now," Carolyn said. "If death happened, I'd have to deal with it. Some cancers are more likely to be fatal than this. We have options."

"Sure we do," I agreed. "It just takes so long to get the show on the road before it's too late and the options run out. I found out I am high risk and the cells are close to the chest wall and if they go through, I'm in deep doo doo! Cancer would have full reign and we'd just be chasing it with chemo and I don't wanna! We're waiting on the insurance now. I want to get on with it. Let's just quit fooling around!"

"Yeah," Carolyn grinned. "Don't deny me my mastectomy! I want it now!"

"And make it snappy!" We both giggled.

"Then we can choose our own styles! This isn't so bad!"

"Yeah, and if we don't like it, we just remodel it."

"Drink your coffee," Carolyn said. "This is morbid."

While it's true that joking about sober things like serious illness or dying seems morbid, it does lighten the spirit to laugh. Through it, I could ask God to help me to overcome my frightened emotions and smile and laugh instead because He is good.

"You have put gladness in my heart …" (Ps. 4:7). Yes, God had given me joy and laughter as a gift from Him. It was OK to be laughing, even in the midst of cancer. God enjoys our laughter and feels pleasure in it.

"For You alone, O Lord, make me dwell in safety" (Ps. 4:8b). God gives us gifts of encouragement as we go through those difficult times. Those faith jars are varied. Maybe it is a friend, like Carolyn, to share the experience. Maybe it is a book, or a song. If we just look for those gifts all along the way, we will find them.

I knew He would never leave me. I knew He would help and strengthen me. I knew He would hold me up with His hand.

At the same time, I struggled with wanting my own plan that would not take me through painful places. I was pretty sure I wouldn't like the current plan, and it worried me. Still, and it wasn't easy to find this jar of faith, I determined to trust Him with cancer.

Carolyn's and my next coffee journey was to the reconstruction surgeon. It is amazing what can be done in today's medicine. I'm sure glad I live in the here and now instead of years ago when my diagnosis would have been a death sentence, but not before total mutilation occurred. Carolyn and I chose different routes of reconstruction and we supported one another through our surgeries. God has given us our lives.

Panglossian

At work a group of us get a word for the day on our computers in the mornings. We have a great time throwing unlikely words around in the office. One day the word was *panglossian*. This is a great word. It means to have an overly optimistic outlook; maybe even glib. I adopted this word. The more I thought about it, the more I was convinced that it was the perfect attitude. I had a God who could do anything so why shouldn't I be *panglossian*?

That favorite mentor of mine, Oswald Chambers, said, "This is the unshakable secret of the Lord to those who trust Him—I will give thee thy life."[2] What a life! Adventure! Surprise! Chambers went on to explain that as soon as you begin to think, "what about this? It means you have not abandoned, you do not really trust God ... when you do get through to abandonment to God, you will be the most surprised and delighted creature on earth; God has got you absolutely and has given you your life."[3]

It's funny; we worry about what we will have to give up if we give God our lives. We don't even wonder what we will *get* in return! And what we get when we give God our lives is a thousand times better than what we are clutching in our fists.

I wanted to witness a miracle. It could come through natural means, that would be OK with me, but I wanted to see God do something big.

I am a believer in community. Before surgery, I was very blessed both at church, in my family, and at work. Meals were arranged, flowers and cards came, and elders and beloved friends anointed my head with oil and prayed. Who but a wonderful, giving Father could put together such care so lovingly and tenderly? I knew the everlasting arms held me, keeping me safe forever in His heart.

This Side of the "Magic Line"

What a relief! After a lengthy surgery to do both a second mastectomy and the double reconstruction, the doctors told me we could not have waited any longer. Cancer had been creeping toward the "magic line," but we got there before cancer did! Neither radiation nor chemotherapy would be required. I praised God for his mercy.

A friend gave me Psalm 16 to read. In this gift I found jars of faith that I could carry with me. As I trust in God, He is my inheritance. He maintains me. He gives me counsel, and I bless Him. He is there in my night seasons and always there before me. My heart rejoices and my flesh rests in hope. He shows me the path of life and His presence is my joy.[4] I imagine that these jars came in crystal, trimmed in gilt, and maybe even had hummingbirds, butterflies, and flowers painted on some of them. They consisted of oil based paint, of course. God is all these things to me, and through this journey, I had plenty of opportunities to look for faith jars! His healing oil poured over my body. I am grateful!

Anita, who now resides in heaven, is the beloved sister of my dear friend, Arlie. Breast cancer sent Anita to the arms of her Savior. At the time she was enduring surgery on this earth, a note was sent to her that said, "There is hope. That's what I want you to know. God has promised us that He holds us in His hands and He has planned for us a hope and a future. If ever that scripture has meaning, it is at a time like this. After surgery remember that you are still beautiful. Everyone has ugly scars. Life gives them to us. Some are on our bodies, some are on our spirits, but the scars are not who we are. When you look at yourself, remember you are beautiful and God loves you."

Anita's beauty endured both before and after her surgery. She embodied encouragement to those around her, even in her journey home to Jesus.

My lovely friend, Stella, who suffered through breast cancer, once asked me if I thought her morbid for planning her own funeral. I assured her that I did not think it morbid. She faced that eventuality sooner than most of us. Stella was very beloved in the community. Besides her place as wife and mother, she had walked with many in their life's journeys. She was a teacher as well as a mentor. She showed others how to trust God through her own sufferings. Even through cancer, the light in her soul still drew others to Jesus. Talk about jars of faith, Stella certainly had hers lined up!

When the time came to celebrate her new life in heaven, those who came could see the glory of the God she loved and the beauty of her life.

With each beloved friend who receives a new diagnosis of breast cancer, I am in awe of the courage each woman shows as she makes life changing decisions. I see the faithfulness of our Father over and over.

I don't know why it is that I am healed on this earth to die another day and some of my dear friends have lost this very battle I have just fought. Yet in losing their earthly lives, they have found the ultimate healing and are home now forever. Who truly has the greater gift?

Only Eternity

Looking back on this sacred journey, I see where God knocked out all my props so that I would look to Him to be my all in all. Where I thought I was alone, He came alongside in the guise of a caring friend or a cool summer evening breeze as I watered my beloved flowers. It could have been His fingers softly stroking my hair as I stroked the hair of my children when I wanted to comfort them.

At times I felt alone and wanted to quit because it hurt in the dark. If you are there, keep going. Be encouraged; God is with you. He will work it out. He will walk alongside you and protect you. Fix your eyes on Him fully and not on anyone or anything around you.

As a cancer survivor with a rearranged body, I have a greater understanding of the faithfulness of God and a peek into heaven. What He has prepared for us there, after we have endured here, is more than wonderful.

Sacred journeys are made up of times and seasons. They are just that—times and seasons—carefully crafted to shape us into His image, and He is glorified. God takes us where the battles are, and when they are done, it's on to the next battle until He calls us home to heaven.

Nothing is forever except eternity.

CHAPTER NINE

DISCOVERY

Discovery, Truth, and Freedom

Therefore if the Son makes you free, you shall be free indeed.
(John 8:36)

What's That You Said?
    I settled back in my chair at Nancy and Wayne's home after attending our Christmas party from work with them and my friend, Derrick. The party was a blast. We sang carols on a hay ride, ate dinner, line danced, and just had a general whopping good time. Now we were settling in for a late night "spot of tea" and chat, just catching up as friends do who haven't seen each other in a while.

God has an interesting sense of plot. When He writes a story, He puts in the most unexpected twists. My mind and body were at rest as I listened to my friends share old times and bring each other up to the present.

I sipped my tea and listened as Derrick asked Wayne, "I haven't seen you in such a long time. What are you doing these days?"

Wayne answered, "I am pursuing my interest in counseling."

"What kind of counseling?"

"Counseling from the spiritual aspect of working with believers in uncovering areas of unforgiveness, sowing and reaping, judgments, vows, and generational sin."

"What does that mean?"

Wayne sipped his tea and set his cup aside. He leaned forward slightly as he explained. "Often Christians struggle with areas of their lives that they have no idea why they're encountering these problems. We have found that in a child's formative years, many judgments, vows, expectations, and wrong beliefs may be made, and the child forms habit patterns and ways of coping and acting out in his or her life—defense mechanisms—that influence the behavior later in life."

Derrick asked, "Is there an area of particular interest that you want to be working with? Are you doing marriage counseling or something else?"

Wayne relaxed, "Well, I have found that I am drawn to people who have been sexually abused."

"Why have you been drawn to working with this kind of abuse?"

"I have discovered that people who have been sexually abused are more real and know that their world has forever been changed and they are seeking genuine healing."

Derrick sipped his tea and set his cup down. "That sounds like a very difficult area in which to work."

"You have no idea! There is an area of severe abuse that causes a person to dissociate."

"What does that mean?"

"Dissociative Identity Disorder, formerly known as Multiple Personality Disorder, is a creative way for children to escape severe trauma abuse."

I was thinking how interesting that subject sounded. I remembered watching a movie called "The Three Faces of Eve" some years ago, starring Joanne Woodward and Lee J. Cobb, concerning multiple personalities. It impressed me.

Wayne continued, "These are difficult days and there is more awareness now of trauma than even ten years ago. It usually begins in childhood before the personality forms and settles. Trauma occurs and the soul believes it cannot survive and splits off. It sort of 'escapes'. Then, another trauma happens and the escape happens again and so on."

I thought back to Dean's childhood and the abuse and trauma that he had endured in his family and the "fallout" I had lived with for so many years.

As Wayne explained further the conditions for DID, suddenly I flattened into the sofa and started shaking as I recognized those conditions in Dean's family and his past. I was surprised that no one seemed to notice anything out of place with me since my mind was bouncing all over the place with reaction.

It kept pressing on me that Dean could have been one suffering from multiple personalities. "That is too unbelievable!" I kept telling myself. "Everybody will think I am crazy for sure if I said something like that!"

Except, as Wayne and Derrick continued conversing, I became more and more convinced. While Wayne talked, I could certainly understand how Dean, as a very young child, may have thought he could not survive any of those traumas—let alone *all* of them.

My mind was going *click click click* running through scenes. Secrets I could not fathom were beginning to fall into place for me. For instance, why couldn't we—any of us connected to Dean—find a place to penetrate into his personality? Even his own wife and children had no clue as to who he was. Could it be that there were so many layers of personalities that we could not find his core—the real Dean?

How was I going to approach this with my children? Could I even accept that this could be true, myself? Who would believe it?

Love and Snot Noses

One time, after I got home from work, Dean told me that he had asked God why He would want him, Dean. His life was hopeless, he was helpless in it, and he could not figure out why God would want him.

At that point our son, Jeff, who was only about two years old, got up from a nap and padded out to stand in front of his daddy. His brown curls were tousled, his shirt wrinkled above his sagging diaper, his blankie wrapped around his shoulders and bunched in his hand as he sucked his thumb. Solemn moppet eyes gazed at his dad.

As a parent, how do you see *your* children?

Has one of your children ever stood before you like Jeff did before his daddy?

What do you want to do with him?

God our Father sees us that way.

How about when he gets a little older and he is asking all those "why" questions? Will they *never* stop? Finally, you say in exasperation, "because I said so!" The little one shrugs and says "OK" and goes about his play.

Have you ever heard God say, "because I said so!"

Your child gets a little older yet and he screws up. Does he cease to be your child? Do you stop loving him? Do you administer discipline, not to harm him, but in hopes of perfecting him?

Have you ever felt the hand of God in discipline?

Whether or not our children disobey, run away, become high achievers, make us cry, or make us proud, it does not matter. They are still our children and we love them.

We have a Father who, in all points, loves us. He has provided a way through Jesus, His First Born, in whom He is well pleased, to gather us into His arms for eternity.

This is good news. Dysfunctions will not exist in heaven. God our Father has promised us a new way of being. He has promised us forever living; He has anointed us with truth; He gives us confidence to move forward even through difficulties; He has given us a clear conscience as we continually go before Him with our earthiness; He has given us cleanliness on the inside; He has given us a deeper ability to love those around us, even through the sweat and the tears. If you don't believe me, just read it for yourself in His great love letter to us, the Bible. This particular list comes out of 1 John in the New Testament.

Our Father sees our moppet eyes, our thumbs wrapped around our snot noses, smells our dirty diapers, and He loves us.

Confidence in Asking

"Now this is the confidence that we have in Him, that if we ask anything according to His will, He hears us. And if we know that He hears us, whatever we ask, we know that we have the petitions that we have asked of Him" (1 John 5:14, 15).

Now that I know my Father in heaven loves me and made a way for me to come to Him, snot nose and all, I can have confidence to come before Him with my requests.

Just as I want to give good things to my children when they ask me, I found that my Father in heaven wants to do the same with me. I can have confidence in my relationship with Him that if He has promised me something, He will deliver it. He cares about my development and how I can resemble His First Born Son, Jesus.

I sought truth and healing. I thought this would be according to God's will. By the stripes of Jesus we are healed, and I wondered how healing could happen if confusion still gripped the past. So after Dean passed away, I asked God to tell me the truth about what was wrong with him. I felt I needed to know.

If God is our Father and wants to give us good things, and we ask according to His will, then He must be listening. He says He will hear us. When I asked for the truth concerning Dean, I prepared to wait. If obedience of faith is pleasing to God, then I would exercise faith and wait for that answer. I would believe God heard me. I knew, too, that He would be good to answer only when the time would be right and I would be able to work with what I learned. He would tell me when He could trust me to walk through the truth with Him, even if it seemed improbable, even if I did it imperfectly but willingly.

He will give us the answers we need to grow into grace, healing, and the image of His First Born. We ask according to His will; He hears us; He answers us.

I figured God would tell me in His own good time. Now was the time. I just never expected something as severe as multiple personality, but it certainly was a fit!

Layers and Personalities

I ran Dean's layers through my mind. *They were personalities?* It made so much sense. Poor tortured man! No wonder he kept saying life felt hopeless.

Just a few years after marrying Dean, I knew something was different about him. I never had any experience with addictions or mental disorders. While my family was not perfect, I did not understand what violent, continual abuse could do to a person, or how it could work out in the life of the abused person.

The more I read and studied, the more sense it made. I could look back on different incidents and times in this light, and it fit. So many changes could happen in him in just a few hours. I found myself wondering "who *is* this?" Was he a collection of personality fragments? And how could he ingest his drugs and then suddenly act normal, with no sign of being under any substance influence and able to do an activity? That always puzzled me. I thought nobody would believe me if I told them that happened.

Maybe this could explain why no routine was ever established at home. Some of the personalities were morning people, some were night owls, and some were just children who needed a grown-up to tell them to go to bed. Maybe this could explain how Dean could look and move like a shrunken old man who needed his cane to get around, then the next day, he might be Mr. Take Charge, who knew his own mind and where he was going—or he might have the wide eyed, fresh faced look of a child discovering his world. Of course, there was the addict, too.

Words like "manic depressive," "bi-polar," and "psychotic" were thrown at Dean during his lifetime. I didn't understand what those words meant, but as I listened to that conversation about multiple personality, well—*this* was familiar territory! I recognized this. It explained the layers.

I started counting up how many different Deans I had known. In my shock, that night of the Christmas party, I realized that I had named some of them over the years. I used to think, "OK, who is he today?" and when it became obvious, I would think, "Well, it looks like it's The Little Boy today," or "The Old Man," or … whoever. I knew he had been broken, but I didn't understand what that brokenness actually meant. What was even more surprising was the realization that my children and I adjusted to the personalities as they came without even thinking about it. It wasn't relationship-based, merely accommodating.

Nobody had to tell me that confusion reigns in persons suffering with multiple personalities and those who live with them. When "nobody is home" and yet "everybody is there" in one body, how can it be otherwise? How can family members relate? Nobody is present long enough in that one body to have a relationship with, just layer after layer. Confusion is paramount, frightening, maddening, and constant.

What Is Dissociative Identity Disorder?

I struggle to understand what Dissociative Identity Disorder (DID) is and how it works. It seems the more I learn, the more levels there are to learn about, and the more difficult it is to learn. I am unknowledgeable and untrained in these matters, but I am a seeker of truth for my family and myself. What little I have gleaned at this point of my studies seems to confirm to me that my husband, Dean, did suffer with DID. My purpose in this chapter is to show what we, as a family, went through, what we learned, and how God saw us through it.

I would ask the forgiveness of those who may be reading this who are knowledgeable and/or may be in the process of healing for my bumbling efforts at explanation. If you are among those who may need more information than I will give here, I recommend that you contact Restoration in Christ Ministries, or other resources found in the Appendix of this book. They are the ones who are knowledgeable.

Tom and Diane Hawkins are the founders of Restoration in Christ Ministries, a non-profit organization begun in 1994 to work with survivors of Dissociative Identity Disorder. They have been through the difficulties of DID themselves. Restoration in Christ Ministries does seminars and has many resources available through the ministry.

In Diane's book *Multiple Identities—Understanding and Supporting the Severely Abused*, she describes DID in this way:

> DID is a unique psychological condition in which the mind splits itself into multiple identities in order to cope with overwhelming childhood trauma. Amnesic barriers are generally erected between the alter-identities, or "alters," who are formed to enable some parts of the person to be sheltered from the reality of the abuse and thus able to maintain a sense of normalcy in an otherwise intolerable situation. These shielded identities are then able to function in everyday life without being encumbered with the effects of the trauma.

Only a very immature psyche will respond to extreme trauma by creating separate identities. Therefore, DID occurs only in individuals whose trauma *began* before the age of 5 or 6. Once the psyche initiates this type of defense, however, it can continue to create more alter-identities throughout life—whenever it serves a beneficial purpose.

Rather than being a true mental illness, DID actually represents a marvelously creative defense mechanism employed by extremely traumatized children. When they had no way of *external* escape, they found a way to escape the intolerable events *internally.* The condition bears the negative connotation of "disorder" only because its smooth operation often breaks down later in life. Disturbing memories, emotions, and behaviors begin seeping through weakened dissociative barriers, interfering with normal daily living and alerting the unsuspecting Host identity that something is wrong. This is what usually motivates survivors to seek help.[1]

When I saw *The Three Faces of Eve* some years ago, I thought it was a strange and exciting story. In the 1950s a young woman in Georgia had been diagnosed with three personalities, and this story told how, through her therapy, she became a united personality. I have heard since, that this film was based loosely on a real story that was not nearly so simple as the screen portrayed.

Also, I have learned since, stories like this are not so rare or strange as I thought. Exciting? That depends on your definition of "exciting!"

For me, learning about the unique aspects of this disorder and how it is employed by gifted and creative individuals has been an incredible journey.

This is something you always think happens "out there." I'm never quite sure where "out there" actually is, but it always happens to someone else. Not me!

This time, incredibly, it seems it *is* me—or at least in my household. I certainly needed my Father's heavenly hand to hold me through this one. He sent me two dear friends, Nancy and Wayne Bentz, to walk alongside me, pray with me, explain things to me, give me tools to work with in trying to understand dynamics I spent a lifetime experiencing. It has helped immensely to see how my life and the lives of my children have been shaped by how we related to Dean.

Diane Hawkins points out that prolonged abuse carried out against a person, usually as a child, can result in DID. She listed several specific situations through which this could occur: pedophile groups, child pornographers, and child prostitution rings. However, any child subjected to sexual exploitation or other severe trauma early in life may develop this condition.2

Satanic Ritual Abuse (SRA) is a predominant cause in which perpetrators deliberately use trauma to create DID in order to bring children under the control of the cult leaders. More information about this can be obtained by making use of the resources listed in the Notes.

In Jim Friesen's book *Uncovering the Mystery of MPD*, he says:

> It is widely known that abused children develop a strong loyalty to the abusing parent. That is part of the problem. Some of the child alters have unrealistically strong bonds to the evil parent(s) … To come to terms with evil in one's parentage is perhaps the most difficult and painful psychological task a human being can be called on to face. Most fail and so remain victims.[3]

Now I understand why Dean could never seem to recover from the childhood abuse he received.

Friesen goes on to talk about Jesus, explaining that the true family is the family of God. While an earthly family may do damage, God provides an eternal family bound by the ties of the Holy Spirit. This healing and health is possible.

Going Deeper

Terri Clark in her book, *More Than One*, lays out this definition: "Dissociation is the ability to 'tune out' from the circumstances around you, and multiple personality disorder evokes the ultimate use of dissociation." She says that, "people with this disorder are not insane, but they are often afraid they are because their world makes no sense."[4]

I can certainly relate to this. Dean's world made no sense to him or to us. Understanding that this is "normal" for DID, it makes sense that life made no sense—erratic behavior, losing things (and blaming the rest of us for that!), losing time, crisis to crisis living, daily craziness, sudden unexpected changes in behavior with or without substance abuse involved, and it explains the layers where I never could seem to get to the bottom to know him. I knew that underneath the layers was this nice guy who was kind hearted, funny, talented, and very smart, but I could never quite reach him. I just knew he was there. Somewhere. Underneath.

I can't begin to say how wonderful it is to find something that *does* make sense of all of this. I believe it is an answer from God.

Terri Clark talked about a debate concerning differences between mental illness and mental disorder. DID is a "dysfunctional way of living," so mental illness has been considered. However, it is more "unique and adaptive and therefore should not be referred to as a mental illness but rather as a unique giftedness." It is "primarily a special learned response that becomes a lifelong coping mechanism to any threatening situation." She says it has been very important for her patients to understand the distinction between illness and disorder.

I would certainly agree with this as I remember how obstinate Dean was about not finding help because he was too worried that he might be found out to be mentally ill and that was too frightening to consider. I used to think he was just stubborn about getting help. After all, if you have a problem, you go get help, get it fixed, and go on with life, right?

No, it's not so simple. I wonder now if his "multiple" system had to protect itself from discovery? Could it be that if steps were taken for change, then the coping mechanism he had built up all his life would fail and that would be too devastating? Of course it was in the process of unraveling anyway, but it was all he knew.

Jim Friesen, who is a director of a counseling center in California, said, "Those who have learned to know these people have been forced to grow, too, and to think in new ways." He is *so* right. My children and I did learn to adapt to whoever Dean was at any given time in relating to him. We never thought about it, it was sort of like a reflex action. We might be doing a project with him and then he would not be interested anymore so we would just carry on without him. The same would happen with conversations, or activities, or plans … didn't everybody live this way?

I think that once the understanding of DID occurs, it could be quite an adventure to live, knowing there could be a reward of healing and not just mindless existing.

Friesen talks about one of his clients, Beth, whose husband was very supportive when he was apprised of her diagnosis. He learned to talk and interact with each of her alters and this helped to speed along her progress toward recovery.

I look back and see how I was often angry with Dean's childish behavior or frustrated with him when he would be bent over, leaning on his cane. Then because I was so often "in charge" (somebody *had* to be!), when he would try to make decisions, I would balk because I knew tomorrow he would be incapable of carrying out that decision. I was usually right the next day. If only I could have had the tools to work with those alters, how different life might have been for all of us!

Friesen talks about one of his clients having a Shepherd to guide her. As I read that, I began to weep because Dean had no shepherd to guide him through his own maze. Almost immediately I heard the still, small voice whisper in my mind, *yes, Child, Dean did, indeed, have a Shepherd.* So—even though no one on earth knew the desperate places that Dean lived, the Eternal Shepherd walked beside him.

I knew then that when I had found Dean's lifeless body that night, Father God had been with him.

Light on the Journey

I have learned that different alters are created to handle different situations. Not all of them are aware of the others.

Terri Clark said, "As inventions of the creative mind of the multiple, alters are essentially *tools* used by the multiple for protection."[5]

I noticed that the therapists asked their clients to "map out" their alter systems. As I studied some of those maps, I thought of different alters I had observed in Dean. It seemed a large list to me. I don't know what might be there if he were on this earth today, but several came to my mind. It relieved me to see so many of my questions answered as I consider the list.

DID looks like this to me: a person is multi-talented and completes a multitude of tasks. The multiple, who also is multi-talented, switches personalities to complete the same multitude of tasks.

Often I would be exasperated at made-up stories or what I perceived as lies from Dean. Jim Friesen explains, "There may be confabulated stories, made up by child alters who are accustomed to turning out explanations to fit any situation. They are great at covering up when they are in charge, with no idea of what just happened. At such moments it is very helpful to be in the presence of non-confrontive people, who understand enough about MPD to take things in stride."[6]

This was another piece to fall into place. Confabulated stories— yes—I would shrug and chalk it up to addict behavior. This was why I found myself acting in the capacity of a mother figure to him quite often. I can name several child parts including a toddler. This was disconcerting, to say the least. Now I understand better. I wish I could have understood then. It seems that many multiples have several child alters.

I can imagine Jesus comforting those children, *I am here, Child. My arms are open wide to you. Run to Me. I am your Safe Place. I will never leave you nor forsake you, nor let you down. You can rest in My love. You can believe in My faithfulness. I am here for you. I will always be here for you. Bring your sorrows to Me, and rest your head on My chest. I will comfort you. Shhhh ... you are Mine.*

Discovering that a high percentage of multiples experience health problems and substance abuse problems was a relief to me. It could also be true that the multiple system could contain a hypochondriac alter. This often confused me. Dean had real health issues and some that weren't so real. I used to think he was a hypochondriac in between the real health episodes. Maybe it was so.

As I read, I saw a recurring theme everywhere. People who developed Dissociative Identity Disorder are very gifted and creative people. I have to agree.

I was aware of Dean's giftedness, but it frustrated me because it seemed to me that his gifts and talents were so often wasted. He would astonish everyone with abilities he would display. In spite of his health, addictions, and mental disorder, he managed to get a degree in electronics (one of those alters was pretty determined!), he designed and supervised the building of a garage, he designed and supervised the installation of a sprinkler system in our yard, he was very creative in woodworking design, he could cook the yummiest meals, and then the next day not know how to do any of those things.

I thought he was just wasting his talents through addictions.

I never thought that perhaps his gifts and talents were being used in ways I could not begin to surmise. How much energy must go into just living day to day when there are several selves to manage! Especially if you thought you had to keep this secret because people would think you were crazy!

I guess I needed to give him a break.

It is good to use caution when telling people DID is a part of your family experience. Relief feels good when the truth is out and the secrets are gone and the bizarre behavior is explained. Still, because of the nature of this disorder, you may not be believed. Friends or family may be angry, or decide they no longer want to know you.

Wayne was quick to point out that this is an area where the church has greatly misunderstood people. When personalities show themselves, they have often been mistaken for demons. This has been very harmful. I can see why this might have been one reason for Dean to stay away from church. He might have been fearful that a switch would happen there and be mistaken. I know one of his alters loved Jesus. After he passed away, I found several highlighted places in his Bible. I don't remember seeing him even reading it! But even that alter did not go to church.

Demonic activity may be present with a multiple system, but it is not part of the person's humanity, and the demon must be dealt with separately from the person's humanity. Just recognizing this is difficult for most Christians who only have a framework for seeing extra activity in a person to be demonic. It may not be so.

I am amazed at these things I am still in process of learning. I am amazed at the cleverness of humankind. I am amazed at the heights of love and glory. I am amazed at the depths of ugliness and darkness. I am amazed at the resiliency displayed by many of us as we travel through this life. I am amazed at our Creator, who formulated us.

Who can fathom the Mind of God? Who can go to the heights where He is? Who can go to the depths where He is? All of these things are known to Him who made us. Nothing is a surprise to Him. Still He calls us to this sacred journey with Him. We don't get it. We may not like it. We may encounter the biggest surprises, but still, He calls us to continue to go forward where we cannot see.

What Gatekeeper?

I think that in the last four years of Dean's life, his gatekeeper left his post, and the revolving door of his multiple system kept going around and around and around. Craziness can't begin to describe those four years. For sheer excitement I don't think it could be beat. I didn't need to travel anywhere for thrills—just go home!

However, in the midst of the frightening times, flashes of humor presented some light moments. Sometimes living with a multiple can give you some great stories!

I usually loved it when the cook showed up, except that it could get expensive. The $300 chicken was delicious. He had cooked it in some air and water roasting contraption. It was state of the art something! I didn't understand how it worked at all, but dinner was wonderful. He never used that machine again.

One time I got home and Dean was cooking dinner and humming. What a nice sound! As soon as I sniffed the air, I knew I was in trouble. He loved hot food as in "burn your tongue" hot food. He'd been growing salsa peppers all summer. This night he put together a zucchini, onion, and salsa pepper mix to put over rice. We sat at the table (which was not customary) and after the blessing (which I knew I was going to need) I took a bite. Yep. Sure enough my tongue burned off and I could feel the steam rushing out my ears and nose.

I said calmly (a feat), "It's a little hot."

Disgusted, Dean said, "Oh, cut it out. It's not either." Then he took a bite. I could see the steam coming out his ears, too. He got up from the table with his plate and tossed over his shoulder, "We need to throw this out."

I smirked. At least I tried to smirk. My mouth still hurt too much.

Once after a meal Dean had cooked, I asked him about going back to school to learn cooking. He couldn't go back to his old profession, due to his physical injuries, but he loved to cook so it seemed like a great idea to me. He agreed that he had thought about being a cook.

I was excited that maybe this could be something to which Dean could turn his energies. At this point in his life he had no profession. The next night when I got home, he was in his chair in the basement as usual. I asked him if he had thought more about cooking school. His response was, "Oh, I don't want to do that." Sigh.

Now if the cook could have been more permanent, that was one alter I could live with happily!

What Manner of Love

"What manner of love the Father has given us that we should be called the children of God" (1 John 3:1).

Picture Jesus rolling down the hill along with several little children. He's laughing, and they are giggling with delight that this grown-up is taking time to play with them. When they reach the bottom of the hill, the little ones jump up and all rush to "pile" on Jesus, who tickles them. Imagine those squealing, squirming little bodies all atop of the grown-up, who is reaching as far as He can for each one.

Suddenly other grown-up hands start to pull them off and tell them to go away and stop bothering the Master.

Jesus sits up, still holding children close to Him. He looks at His disciples and says, "The Kingdom of God is made up of children with hearts like these. Let the children come to Me."

What manner of love …

Our Father God holds us in His love. He has bestowed on us the great gift of His heart. When we laugh, He delights in our laughter and booms out His own laughter. When we are broken, He is broken with us.

He tells us that when we belong to Him, He works in us to change us to look like Him. Children resemble their parents. All the inherited traits are bestowed upon little ones in the womb. The physical features are bestowed in the secret place of formation.

God is Spirit. When He brings us into His family through His First Born Son, Jesus, He sets about bestowing His traits on our spirits. The unseen part of us.

It is not revealed to our mortal eyes. Some of us are quite broken and the healing may take a lot of time. But our identity in *all* its facets is open to the molding of our heavenly parent. He is designing a new identity. He is pulling all the pieces together to form the image of His First Born Son in all His children.

As His image takes form in us, we begin to hold our heads up. We can lift our faces to the Son Light and feel the caress of our Father's hands on our faces as His love cascades into our souls. Take a deep breath and let Him fill the dark places!

God's Word says if we walk in the light as He is in the light, then we can love one another and our love is pure and true. Darkness passes away and the Son shines brightly and we see him as He is.

It is safe to laugh when Jesus plays with us. It is safe to love when our Father God has His hands on our faces. It is He who stands between us and the broken things.

Just as we long to give good things to our children, He longs to give good things to us—only we don't believe Him.

He promises us eternal life to be lived in the Son Shine. He promises us a new identity in Him—the Image of Jesus stamped on our very beings. His Word tells us that He chose us for love and that He *is* that Love and He invites us to abide in Him.

As we learn to trust His words given in the Bible and live according to what He says, He takes us step by painful step to the place of real healing.

Overcoming

"For whatever is born of God overcomes the world. And this is the victory that has overcome the world—our faith. Who is he who overcomes the world, but he who believes that Jesus is the Son of God?" (1 John 5:4, 5)

Overcoming! Believing! Faith! Victory! Freedom!

Are not these the earmarks of life as we want to live it?

I asked God to tell me the truth. I thought I needed to know. After realizing that Dissociative Identity Disorder seemed to fit so well, I wished that Dean could have been diagnosed in his lifetime. I believe we would have found him to be suffering with DID. Could I have been more effective in helping him had I known then? Or would it have been more frightening to stay with him had I known? Faith!

What a relief it was to realize there is a name and a treatment for this disorder and an explanation for the confusion that wrapped around my life. Mixed emotions came along with the knowledge. Mourning and compassion replaced anger and bitterness. Also a great sorrow that Dean was not diagnosed and treated for this disorder. Hope was available but we had been unaware of it. The lost opportunity on earth has given way to complete healing for Dean in heaven. Once again—the Cross is the place to lay down things that can only remain unfinished on earth—but wholly healed in heaven for all eternity. Victory!

I believe I have God's assurance that Dean is in heaven and my labor was not in vain. He is now the soul he was meant to be, integrated into a healthy whole that is able to trust and worship his Creator forevermore! God is good, all the time, no matter what. Believing!

While Dean's healing has occurred in heaven, learning about Dissociative Identity Disorder and recognizing how it fit Dean brought much healing to me here on earth. God used Dean's special circumstances to teach and shape me into God's child and the image of His Son. I learned about understanding rather than judging; accepting rather than rejecting; patience instead of temper; loving the unlovely;

looking for the story under the surface. In arriving, there is much failure, and I have learned about the art of waiting.

Overcoming!

Coming out to a bright new morning after a long dark night feels unbelievably wonderful! God's love and His life will always overcome death in its every form.

Free Indeed!

CHAPTER TEN

REFLECTION

Reflecting the Character of God

So God created man in His own image; in the image of God He created him; male and female He created them. (Gen. 1:27)

The sign said "4.1 miles" and an arrow pointed the way. Several extended family members were camping for a long weekend and decided a hike would be in order. I liked hiking and being out in God's beautiful nature, but … four miles! And one way!

Actually we cheated. We drove a vehicle to the other end of the lake so we could ride back. The four miles didn't look so intimidating anymore and we set out.

The woods were warm and fragrant in the late spring day. Birds twittered warnings of our coming to each other in the gently swaying trees. Critters scurried in the underbrush around us. At some points we slid as the trail disappeared into rock beds.

Suddenly the path rounded the corner and a beautiful panorama lay before us. The lake came into full view and we stopped hiking just to gaze. The rocks on the other side jutted straight up into the air and looked like they were folded together accordion style. Many appeared flat on top.

The green-blue waters below reflected the rock towers to perfection. It was hard to tell where the rocks ended and the lake began. We could see no boats in the water.

A waterfall dribbled through melting ice somewhere in the midst of the mountains as it made its way to the lake. Mountain crevasses were muted by the sun's rays. A rock island sat in the middle of the lake with a few trees growing on it.

Below us all sizes of rounded rocks lay on the perimeter of the lake and we studied our reflections in the still water. Every rugged rock had its mirror. Every feathery tree was repeated below it. The eagle soaring above had his counterpart, too. It all looked so fresh and innocent, peaceful and free. It appeared as if every secret were exposed and every danger eradicated. No one talked. We just breathed in this perfect moment.

Yet if we had come upon this very spot just a month or two before, we might have seen a frozen waterfall, treacherous cliffs, and rocks lurking in murky depths of white cap waters. Glorious beauty? Maybe, if there were no winds and clouds blowing snows that could freeze body and soul.

Where were the reflections then?

It's amazing how our souls reflect what lies inside of us. We think we are hiding our souls from the world. The truth is that our very actions speak of the state of our hearts and souls.

In the beginning of time, in a perfect world made by a perfect God, the man and woman He fashioned were transparent and reflected His own image. God said it was good.

Then the evil serpent appeared and invaded the purity of their souls. The reflection of God in the man and the woman clouded over and the winter of their souls set in.

We, as the race of mankind, chose another route than what had been given to us. Sin became the norm and our souls were dulled.

Many of us wander far and wide before we accept the provision God made for us through His Son Jesus Christ and we comprehend who we were created to be and set out on a sacred journey to reclaim that inheritance.

Somehow we don't expect the journey to be so difficult. We want to return to that place of pristine beauty, but we quickly realize that the path is full of rock slides to try us.

As the process of that shaping happens in us, we harden our hearts. We do that because to be shaped, by its very definition, means to be pounded, prodded, pulled apart, slapped together, tossed around, and slammed to the table. What next? We wonder. This is not what we signed up for when we went to the Cross of Christ on our knees. Life was supposed to get better and not worse. We were told that He had a wonderful plan for our lives and all that.

A little refrain runs through our minds—something about being a living sacrifice. Is there no other way?

Refuge and Fortress

Yes, of course there is another way, but it is not the way of the sacred journey to restore our souls. We fear we do not recognize the work of God in us as disasters seem to disable us. Can Light be trusted or will another blow come out of the dark? We begin to build fortresses around ourselves.

A fortress is a fort—a fortified place, a military defense. In the Middle Ages a fortress would consist of a keep, which is the tower in the center where life was nurtured, and the courtyard where the town bustled, surrounding the keep. Along the walls would be stables and other needs of the society within the fortress. Sentries were posted on the ramparts above for constant lookout for enemies. Gates lifted and lowered as people came and went. It was no easy task to do war against such a fortress. It was often a refuge for the inhabitants. A refuge is a place of shelter and protection against danger.

The rocks around that lake looked like a fortress. It would seem like a place where an enemy could not penetrate. A place made by the hand of God. Refuge and fortress usually refer to God's protection of us. However, because we would rather trust our own shelters, the seasons of life batter against them and build ice until the flow of life is held captive like a mammoth in a glacier. As the snows continue, we pack it and pack it around us until we are encased in ice.

We think we are strong, but we are only frozen.

How can we reflect God's character when our hearts are frozen and immobile?

I live on a hill. There is no other way in and out of my neighborhood than the hill in front of my house. During an ice storm last winter, I had a ringside seat to a great winter slip 'n slide show from my living room. A very shiny sheet of ice covered the hill both directions including the cul-de-sac across the street. I watched cars with locked wheels going down every which way but not up. At one point I was sure there would be a pile up at the bottom, but miraculously everyone missed everyone else. I still marvel at that miracle. Twice I ran for my life as cars skidded into my driveway. I quit shoveling snow and decided not to be a part of that show and stayed home from work for a couple days. Until the thaw came, life could not continue as normal.

Breaking Up the Deeps

Nothing is as tragic as a soul whose heart is frozen but believes it is alive. It is like the walking dead. This iced up heart thinks it's protected but it is just blank. It does not despair and that would seem to be a good thing. However this heart does not experience exhilaration either. That can only be a sad thing. Every day is the same. It seems safe. It seems secure. But it's really only frozen in the glacier fortress built around it.

Who can say how much pain it has taken to bury a heart in ice?

One winter our Cub Scout troop went sledding. The icy hill dropped straight down into a park. But the kicker was before you hit the park, you had to clear a huge lip and dip. From the top I watched the kids and some of the adults careen down the hill and fly through the air before slowing to a stop in the park. I didn't have a sled but my neighbor kindly loaned me her old fashioned wooden sled. I started down the hill. As I gained momentum I gripped the sides of the sled. With unhappy surprise I realized that the grips in my hands were in the air and not attached to the sled. Nor was I attached to the sled anymore. Shock wave. The lip and dip loomed and my mouth dried out. Pretty soon I was airborne. I hoped the sled would stay below me. Remarkably I landed with the sled and my hands still grasping the grips in the air.

We think we are safe; then the grips come off. Unexplainable situations arise in our lives and wield a sledgehammer against the ice in our hearts; then shock waves send us struggling through a crisis of belief.

The ice begins to move, it cracks then it grates together. Pieces begin to fall off and melt. Bigger pieces splash into the water below. Before long a trickle of water becomes a tiny waterfall driving rivulets into the once solid ice.

A question invades through the painful melting of our hearts: *Will we believe God?*

Our very living depends upon our answer to this question. Adam and Eve were deceived in the garden by the serpent asking this very question. *Did God really say … ?* The man and woman began to doubt the very word of the One who gave them life, walked every day with them in the cool of the evening, and sustained their very beings. Their decision was *not* to believe. They went against the evidence of their eyes and all of their senses. They were kicked out of the garden so they would not live forever in this evil and fallen state. Winter entered our hearts through them.

Because of God's great love and compassion, He made a way for our redemption through the Cross of Christ.

The challenge comes again: *Will we decide to believe God?* Will we believe that He will do for us and in us all He said He would do?

When Jesus lived on earth, He did many miracles. He healed people. He brought people back to life from the dead. He delivered them from darkness. He answered the deep questions of their hearts and minds. Yet in His own hometown of Nazareth, those He walked with every day were ready to kill Him. After announcing in the synagogue that He had been sent to "heal the brokenhearted, preach deliverance to captives, give sight to the blind, free the oppressed," the Scripture says, "He closed the book and gave it back to the attendant and sat down." Everyone was staring at Him like He had lost His mind. They didn't believe Him.

Again He announced, "Today, this Scripture is fulfilled in your hearing."

They all knew Him as Mary's son and as the local carpenter. I'm sure much of the furniture or tools they used were made by Him. Yet as He claimed to be the Messiah, their wrath stirred, and they rushed Him out of the building and up the street to throw Him off the cliff. He walked right through the midst of them and out of town.

He could not do mighty works among them because of their unbelief.[1]

Believing can be a mighty struggle, especially if we can't see the thing for which we are believing. Oftentimes what we are hoping will come to pass in our lives seems a long time coming. We just can't see it. Jesus cannot do mighty works among us because of our unbelief.

We come back to the debate. *Will we believe* that God knows best? *Will we believe Him* as He said He would do exceedingly abundantly above all we can ask or think?

We were made in the image of God. We cannot reflect the character of someone we will not believe.

If we will determine to step out in risk daily, in spite of all odds, and say "Yes! I believe!"—God *will* move on our behalf. He promises He will.

If we will determine to believe, then we stand on the brink of His glorious adventure for us. Only then are we ready to go where He calls and sends us, without thought for how He will manage it in us. We simply know that He *will* manage it. We have chosen to believe.

It's all I ask, Child, that you give up your plans to Me. Trust Me with everything that is important to you. I love you, I have your best interests at heart. I have a plan that will delight you and I will be delighted to give it to you. Trust Me. Walk with Me. I will guide your every step. I will go before you and be your rear guard. Don't be afraid. I love you. I delight in you, My Child.

It is our Father's great delight to watch us come alive. It is His great delight to fashion a plan that will reach those deep places in us and cause new energy in our souls.

There is no more need to live in winter. The ice breaks and the life flow begins.

Reflecting God's Character

Once again this lovely spring day shows us sitting on a rock above the calm, reflective surface of the water below. Its beauty fills us with peace. We breathe in the fresh, pure air.

The work that God is doing in us is fresh and pure as well. We are beginning to reflect His character in our lives as we grow confident in walking forward.

In the Gospel of John, Jesus says, "By this My Father is glorified, that you bear much fruit; so you will be My disciples" (John 15:8), and "You did not choose Me, but I chose you and appointed you that you should go and bear fruit ... " (John 15:16).

What are some results of the divine "ice melt projects" that are our lives? God's original intention for us in the Garden of Eden was to be made in His image. Has God been successful in remolding us into His image?

Take a look.

He has given us courage to take a stand when the occasion for it arises. It's a risk. But we believe that He will cover our risk and see us through to a wise resolution.

He has given us compassion in loving others. It's a risk. We might be rejected. But we believe that He will love us more completely and will see to any lack that we may endure.

He has given us honor in the face of unfairness or opposition. It's a risk. But we believe that He will uphold us and strengthen us against any force seeking our harm.

He has given us generosity in supporting others with our resources. It's a risk. Not everyone will use our gifts wisely, be they financial or otherwise. But we believe that He will supply our every need.

He has given us glory in creating and following dreams. It's a risk. But we believe that He will carry us even through success and failure to achieve His dreams for us.

He has given us justice and mercy in our dealings with others. It's a risk. But we believe He ultimately holds justice and mercy in His own hand.

It is simply a risk to live. It's a risk to enter into the hearts and lives of those around us. It's a risk to experience each others' tragedies. We may tell a little of the story, we may pray for one another, but the next week we want to hear that things are better.

It's a risk to determine to become equipped to go the distance with one another; yet when we do, we are reflecting the character of God to each other.

As a Father, He is proud of us as we walk in His footsteps and mirror who He is to those around us.

How did we get here? Through the living sacrificing; the struggle through fear to a sound mind that is required to go forward; through learning to trust God's protection in the winter storms of our hearts; in obeying His commands through abiding in His love; grappling with failure and forgiveness; persevering against opposition; contending with death and illness, and coming to believe the truth that God will never leave us nor forsake us.

It is a mystery to us how God inhabits the praises of His people. Wonderful things happen in our spirits when we worship Him. He is worthy of our praise. His peace comes in where turbulence once raged. He gives us His companionship. His pleasure floods our souls. His promises become real. The future holds potential. Life becomes exciting. Fears of aging, dying, and loneliness don't need to ruin the life He gives us. He is our refreshment. Oh, that we could live on the mountaintop!

Joshua told his people to consecrate themselves—clean up their acts—because the next day they would see the Lord do amazing things among them.[2]

I want to see those amazing things!

Reflection in Laughter and Color

I love to laugh. I believe that it is one of those amazing things in this life full of risk. If God did not have a sense of humor and love to laugh Himself, then where did we get laughter? Would little children have been climbing all over Jesus if He was a sourpuss? I don't think so.

Laughter is another reflection of the character of God. It's a gift from Him to us. Remember laughing with someone until you were crying? Didn't that make you feel good all over?

Lord, I love your sense of humor! You are SOOOO funny! *Child, your laughter is music to my ears.* Wow! God loves our laughter? Yes! Just as the laughter of a little child is music to the ears of his parents (and his grandparents!)—so is our laughter music to our Daddy God's ears. Are we special? You bet! We are *very* special to our heavenly Father.

He sent His Son so we could know Him and be like Him. He made us in His image. He's simple.

Huh? You argue. He's *God!* He's immutable, immortal, omniscient, omnipresent; He's from forever and lives forever, on the throne above the universe, God Most High, everlasting …

Yeah, I know. But I can't possibly understand all those things.

Jesus came to show us His heart.

Do you recall the picture of Him playing with the children? Remember that He said that unless we become as a child, we would not know the Kingdom of God? I can understand this simple Man. I can see His heart of love toward me. I can reflect Him because I can see Him. I can put my hand in His.

I like to sit out on my porch on summer evenings. Did I mention that it is an old fashioned wrap-around-the-house porch? Reflections on the character of God are everywhere we care to look. On this particular summer evening, I was captivated by the transformation in the evening sky. I watched God paint the sky with broad strokes. He drew His brush and brilliant pinks, fuchsias, and golds reflected the rays from His throne room. As the brilliance muted, He took His brush again and dabbed a little here, a little there, with little pink billows in gray blue clouds in relief against an azalea-colored horizon. No one paints like our Daddy God! And how He paints our lives so carefully!

CHAPTER ELEVEN

A New Thing

God is Doing a New Thing in a New Life

Do not remember the former things, nor consider the things of old. Behold, I will do a new thing, now it shall spring forth; shall you not know it? I will even make a road in the wilderness and rivers in the desert. (Isa. 43:18, 19)

Moving On

Abraham was a nomad. He didn't start out that way. It appears his family was pretty well established in the land of Ur, which is better known as southern Iraq.

One day Abraham's father, Terah, decided to pull up stakes and move to another city, Haran. It, too, was located in what is modern

Iraq. Terah took two of his sons and their families with him. Then he died in Haran.

I think Abraham could have inherited the family business. He could have employed a lot of people. He could have established himself socially.

While the Bible doesn't say he was a businessman, it does say he owned a lot of stuff, had plenty of servants, and a beautiful wife. That indicates to me Abraham's success. By any standards, Abraham had it all.

Then came the call of God. "Abraham," God said, "I want you to leave your family, your country, your business and social standing and go to a land that I'm not going to tell you about yet. I am going to bless you and make you famous."[1]

Perhaps that sounds strange. It does to me. How would God have talked to a wealthy and successful man in a way that would inspire him to make such a drastic move? He had already moved with his father and re-established his life and household. God was calling him once more. This time the call was to an undiscovered region in that generation. Again Abraham packed up his wife, his wealth, his people, his livestock and headed for parts unknown.

Do you recognize when God is calling you to a new place? Maybe it's a new style of inner living or it could be literally a new place to live, or perhaps both.

Very simply, the realization came that I could no longer stay in the home I had lived in for most of my adult life. I boarded a plane to visit my Mom for Christmas. I was excited to go. We had planned this trip for some time. As soon as the plane left the ground, a huge sigh escaped me. With surprise I understood that it was relief to be away from my home.

I always considered the house to be Dean's. Somehow I had never been able to make friends with it. After he passed away, I tried remodeling to make it my own, but not even the remodeling could make me friends with that house.

This was God's call for me to literally leave the old place and go on to a new place. A place I did not know. A place where I understood the next move was going to be in the dark and only God knew that direction.

God was drawing me on to totally unfamiliar territory. The time arrived to move on—but to where? And how? Have you ever been in a circumstance like this?

Face Like Flint

Seeking the frontier is both adventurous and frightening. We want to know what is beyond our scope, yet we are afraid to step out to find out. It might jump up and overpower us, and we might find ourselves completely out of control and grabbing for air instead of something of substance.

Yet evidences of adventuring are all over history. It was once thought that the earth was flat and if you ventured too far out to sea you'd fall off the earth. Then somebody decided to find out … what if Columbus had not come?

The Pilgrims set out to find a new life in the New World. They didn't know what they would find. Some of them even died. What if they hadn't persisted?

Lewis and Clark, with the help of Sacajawea, blazed a trail across the North American continent that later drew thousands of pioneers in wagon trains known as the Great Migration as they sought to settle into new lives. What if they stayed in their safe homes in the eastern part of the continent and not braved the dangers?

What if Paul had not answered the call on the road to Damascus to become an apostle to the Gentiles and tell people about Jesus? Or what if William Carey had not gone to India? Or Hudson Taylor to China?

What does all this mean to us now?

We are in a familiar place and we have established ourselves. We feel pretty comfortable and we think we know the God we've been serving. Or maybe it's not a matter of comfort, but it's a matter of what we've become familiar with and, therefore, we'll just settle, thank you.

Then we hear a call. At first we can't believe that God would really ask us to change our course right in the middle of our settled life. Even if that life isn't so comfortable, we are used to it and things should go on as they always have. Shouldn't they?

Why would God tell us to leave our communities and go somewhere else?

Oswald Chambers, in *My Utmost for His Highest*, describes a move like this. He talks about Jesus being out in front with His face set like flint. Jesus is suddenly unfamiliar. The way He is leading is unfamiliar. We are afraid and we don't know where He is going. We've never been this way before.[2] Will we follow?

The way we've been relating to God is changing. He is not satisfied with our satisfaction. He put us on this earth to further His kingdom, and He has work for us to do. He's been busy refashioning us for the work.

Now our relationship with Him is changing. We aren't sure what exactly is happening or what to do about it, but we know we cannot go back. We must move on.

Moving on—it's unfamiliar. There is only forward. We know God is before us and somehow, we know He wants us to follow. But He doesn't look the same to us anymore.

A promise echoes through our minds. God is doing a new thing. We can let go of the old things. He is making a new road for us to walk. What will be on that road? He's causing new streams to flow in the deserts of our lives. What new plants will grow there?

Abraham chose to set his face like flint and follow where God led to the new region Abraham did not know. He knew the One who was leading and that was enough for him.

How about you and me? Do we need the roadmap first or will we follow the One who is leading?

The Struggle with "Go"

When a big move of God seems to be coming, count on facing resistance beforehand. Oswald Chambers said, "When God gives a vision and darkness follows, wait."[3]

There's our enemy, the devil, taking our flesh right along with him. However, God has sent His Spirit to assure His ultimate success in our lives no matter how bad it looks on earth. Yes, there are giants in the land. Yes, there is warfare as long as we walk on earth. But we don't need to be weak-kneed and lily-livered. We can go take the land anyway. God gave it to us!

When that sigh escaped me in the airplane, I knew my life was about to change again. When I arrived back home after the trip, I looked around that house and said a mental goodbye. I called my children to tell them what I was planning, and, to my astonishment, they both responded, "Go for it, Mom. I'm so glad you are doing this." I don't know what I expected but it wasn't, "Go for it!"

I set about finding land to build on, and within two weeks I became the proud owner of a lot set in trees with a partial view of a river valley. It felt like home as soon as I saw it. The speed in which this happened confirmed that this was God's gift to me, a new place to start a new life, no longer wrapped in the past. This home would be a stake in the ground and a remembrance of God's faithfulness.

I thought that, because this new venture started so brilliantly, that everything would just fall into order. That's what is supposed to happen when you know you are doing what God is leading you to do. Isn't that so?

As I set about taking apart a household of many years, the remembrances of lost dreams, broken lives, and broken promises swept through right along with the sweeping out of belongings. *I'm here, Child,* I heard. *There are new dreams.*

"Weeping may endure for a night, but joy comes in the morning" (Ps. 30:5).

New doors opened that I must walk through and shut behind me. Old regrets dropped behind the closed doors, and God moved before me with new amazing things. I am blessed and privileged to be His child.

We were talking about resistance and darkness following a vision. I'm sure I'm not the only one who gets bent out of joint when such resistance comes. Somehow a flood happened in the basement of the home I was selling. Wouldn't you know that it happened the night before the Multiple Listing came out and we had to cancel the Realtor Tour. That certainly dampened my expectations for a while! As my daughter used to say, "I felt like to cry." It seemed impossible. Who would buy a house that had flooded? My flood happened as a big mold scare swept the country in the home buying business. I think my house got black balled. We dried it out and repaired all the damage as quickly as we could. Even as despair clouded my vision, I was still aware that God had known this would happen.

Houses in the real estate market were selling like hotcakes—except mine. Yet even in this road in the wilderness, God provided a stream with new plants, just as His Word promised. My builder, designer, and I were putting together the plans for the new house. We met each week, changing the plans, setting walls in and taking walls out. I wanted lots of windows to let in the light and double French doors to open onto the wrap around porch. I dreamed of ministry and guests someday enjoying this new home.

Finally! The day came when my old house sold. Somehow a bogey man had his fingers in that deal, too. Selling the house was a disappointing transaction, and once again I had to trust that God would make up what I lacked.

Anyone who has built a house would know that this is where patience is bred. God's plan was forward motion, but it sometimes seemed that His timing didn't *show* that He planned forward motion. I spent a year in an apartment waiting ... and waiting ... and waiting.

I thought again about the wilderness road and considered in that interim waiting time how God was preparing the new place. It frustrated me that the building of this house took so long. I kept reminding myself that God's timing is always perfect.

Once the house plans were complete, the builder arranged for materials to be delivered. He scheduled his subcontractors to come and assemble those materials. Sometimes one contractor had to wait upon another before his job could be done. One job at a time, the house rose from the ground. Step by step.

As the new house took shape, God built fresh life into my soul. The old must be cleansed, healed, or moved out before the new can move in. Step by step.

In the new place I would still be in process through this fallen life on earth, but no longer chained to the confusion of the past. As the house took shape, so did the change in my soul. Nearly every day I stopped by to watch the exciting progress as a slab grew into sticks, then walls, and a roof went on, and then I chose paint.

At last! Oh happy day! I moved in! I felt at home immediately, and God's presence filled the house.

The rivers flowed. Literally. Within a week of moving in, a flood happened in my brand new guest bedroom. Now this was fishy! *Nobody* has a flood in the house they are selling *and* in the brand new house they just built. One or the other, maybe, but *not* both! Something was fishy-smelly with that!

As we cleaned up the new flood in the new house, we set about dedicating the whole of the premises to God's use. No bad giants allowed! Only rivers of life with new plants could be here.

Even though this house is a stake in the ground, I know it's possible I could lose it one day. Nothing on this earth is certain. Even in the end the whole earth will burn up and the only treasures we will possess will be those we have in Jesus Christ.

Until then … ever moving forward.

Living In Mystery

Larry Crabb, in *Finding God*, said, "It is difficult to enter a reality that we can't see. But when the Spirit opens the door, when we catch a glimpse of the other side, we cannot stay where we've been."[4]

This is so true! Once we have caught a glimpse of a vision that God draws us on to, we just can't fit into the box we once lived in. It is a mystery how going through dark times gives us the courage to step out and go where God leads. We've been stretched and now we are made for new things.

As my friend Carolyn said, "We have tested Him, trusted Him and now we can move on with Him."

Chambers talks about vision and reality. He says that God gives us a vision then He will take us to valleys to bear the blows that will make us ready to walk in the vision.[5] If we will have patience, we will come out and, as God says, all things are made beautiful in His time. It's for real, and once the process has begun, we will never be satisfied to live in the box again.

This spoke to me as I realized that God had given me the vision for this new home and the use of it. Then came along every obstacle in sight, and out of sight, to discourage me and tempt me to give up. However, it is worth every struggle.

I don't know for sure since I have not had the opportunity to interview him, but I would think that Abraham thought the conflicts he endured to receive the blessing from God to all generations was worth every struggle as well.

How wonderful it is that we have a God who plans great things for us, then sends us along just the right route where He can shower us with those great things as we exercise faith. How delighted He is when we step out in that mysterious place where we can't see the road just because He calls us.

I know of your love for Me, Child, and your desire to serve Me. I am pleased with you. I have a plan for you, and I have work for you to do. I will lead you, guide you, walk beside you. I will not leave you alone. I have a future and a hope for you. Trust Me. Wait on Me. Do as I ask and I will shower blessings upon you. I will give you a harvest as you trust Me.

I love living in mystery! God does so much more for me as I follow Him, and the surprises are awesome! Why live any other way?

The Next Thing

In Stephanie Grace Whitson's book, *Secrets on the Wind*, she creates a wonderful character named Granny Max. Granny Max is a sage. She is wise, comforting, and has answers because she is close to God. She is also very practical. I appreciate Granny Max. When in doubt as to the next step to take in a circumstance, Granny Max would tell everyone, "Just do the next thing." I like that. "Just do the next thing." It just might be the dishes.

I would find myself looking back at old photo albums and think, "Dean looked good here," or "he didn't look good here." Sometimes I would think, "This was a fun time."

The best "looking back" is when I can get past those thoughts of the circumstances at the time and instead, remember how faithful God was through it all.

Now I am in the new place. I don't know where He is leading me to go next, but I know that I want to go where He leads.

I work constantly at letting go of former things, of old ways of thinking and old reactions. What was acceptable or necessary before has changed.

If I want to go on a trip at the last minute, I can do it. It is safer now to be spontaneous than ever before. Guard duty is relaxed. It is also easier to make a fool of myself than ever before because the tight restraints that once bound me are gone.

I am free to look forward to doing things I've never done before or been at liberty to do before. I can honor Dean's memory and still move ahead.

God is my Rock. It is safe to let go of the old life. It is over. Dean is in heaven and his race is done. Mine is beginning anew. God said, "*I will do a new thing, now it shall spring forth.*"

A new thing! Wow! In my life! Not a life put on hold for the sake of someone else; someone who needed that life for survival, but a new life without those claims upon it.

It is a new season to feel the freedom that God gives. Freedom to feel joy, and gladness in serving the Lord in new ways. Freedom to use the gifts and talents He has either given me or formed in me over the painful years.

I have become more of a risk taker. I think it came by default, and it overrides the old longing for being safe because taking risks were too dangerous and scary. If I couldn't see what was in the water, I didn't want to rock the boat.

Then came the sacred journey, and the next thing I knew, the boat was rocking and it was none of my doing. I learned to rely on God because those risks were so great. But I have found the rewards of freedom are even greater.

Life can be lived to the full when you are prepared to risk jumping into the unknown even when you are afraid. You can be sure that when you jump, Jesus is always there to catch you. The Spirit of God is ready to equip you, lead you, and show you adventures that are over and above anything you could ever ask or dream. The abundant life! It doesn't come without pain or risk. Taking that step when you don't know where it will lead—that's heroic faith. Then God comes with the rewards. He says so. In the Bible.

I'll never go back to "safe." I can't. If we are to be ready and available when God brings desperate souls to us for healing, relief, and wholeness, "safe" just isn't an option. We are in a war, remember? It will be a struggle to the death to snatch some from the fire as Jude, in the Bible, says, even to the sizzling of our own garments as we get close to the fire (Jude 23).

There is no place of safety except in the Spirit of God. Even so, sometimes it doesn't look too safe where He takes us. But it is the only way to go!

This is the time to seize the next opportunities set before me. I am available for God's purposes. What about you? I wonder what *is* the next thing?

Glory In Heaven

I have heard it said that this life is a preparation for heaven. I think it must be so. In heaven we will be doing His will, praising and enjoying God, and giving Him glory. If we are not doing this on earth first, then heaven will be foreign to us. If we are already walking in the light of splendor and doing those things, then it will be even more glorious when we arrive in heaven.

So—what road are you on? What is the next thing? Where is God calling you to go? What is your great adventure? Will you answer His call? Will you let Him be your all in all through it?

When He comes for you, how will you be found? Will you be doing your own thing? Or will you be about your Father's business?

ABOUT THE AUTHOR

LINDA JO REED IS a writer with a mission: to encourage people to hope. Her message is that life's battles are God's, and He will sustain each person engaged in it with Him.

Linda Jo Reed is a widow, cancer survivor, mother of two, and grandmother of nine boys. She has published stories in two anthologies as well as articles in several periodicals, and she won an Honorable Mention in the 76th Writers Digest short-story contest. Currently working for Partners International, a seventy-year-old global ministry, she manages the Sponsor A Child program. She also speaks at events and retreats. Her website is http://www.lindajoreed.com/.

Like her on Facebook.

NOTES

Chapter One

1. Acts 9:1–9, author's paraphrase.
2. Romans 12:1–2, author's paraphrase.
3. Lewis, *The Lion, the Witch and the Wardrobe,* 86
4. Hugo, *Les Miserables,* 804.
5. Lucado, *God Came Near,* devotional calendar, August 16, 2000.
6. Hoff, B. J., *Thorns & Thrones: Encouraging Words for Faithful Living,* devotional calendar, September 21, 1991.

Chapter Two

1. Genesis 16, author's paraphrase.
2. Chambers, *My Utmost for His Highest,* February 14.
3. Ibid., August 29.
4. Ibid.

Chapter Three

1. Acts 16:25–32, author's paraphrase.
2. Flint, Annie, "He Giveth More Grace," hymn in the public domain.
3. 1 Kings 19, author's paraphrase.

4. Roper, *Our Daily Bread* (Grand Rapids: RBC Ministries, 2004) December 20, 2004.

Chapter Four

1. 2 Samuel 13–19, author's paraphrase.
2. Dan Allender and Tremper Longman III, *Bold Love*, 36.
3. Chambers, *My Utmost for His Highest*, January 1.
4. Ibid., February 6.
5. Allender, *The Healing Path: How The Hurts In Your Past Can Lead You To A More Abundant Life*, 30.
6. Ibid., 21.
7. Ibid., 87.
8. Rios, "Making Me Strong," *Lord, I Believe*, Cassette Tape, © 1988 Diadem Music.
9. Allender, *The Healing Path*, 134.
10. Colossians 1, author's paraphrase.

Chapter Five

1. Ephesians 6:10–18, author's paraphrase.
2. Sheets, *Intercessory Prayer*, 50.
3. Brad Long and Jeanne Kraak, *The Dunamis Course* Student Workbook, 37.
4. Psalm 18, author's paraphrase.
5. Chambers, M*y Utmost for His Highest*, May 8.
6. 2 Kings 8:8–23, author's paraphrase.
7. Peck, *The Road Less Traveled*, 50.

Chapter Six

1. Steve Flora, "Hearing God's Call," sermon based on Samuel 3, preached at Garland Alliance Church, Spokane, WA, May 1, 2005.
2. Hosea, author's paraphrase.
3. Chambers, *My Utmost for His Highest*, February 28.

4. Genesis 3, author's paraphrase.
5. Willard, "Hidden Valleys," *We Believe,* Cassette Tape, © 1991 The Sparrow Corporation.
6. 1 Samuel 25, author's paraphrase.
7. Allender, *Bold Love,* chapter 11.
8. Bosch, *Our Daily Bread,* (Grand Rapids: RBC Ministries, 1995), January 3, 1995.
9. Flora, "Hearing God's Call."
10. Beattie, *The Language of Letting Go: Daily Meditations For Codependents,* 41–42.
11. Ibid.
12. Ibid.
13. Ibid.
14. Crabb, *Finding God,* 61.

Chapter Seven

1. Sittser, *A Grace Disguised: How The Soul Grows Through Loss,* 180.
2. 2 Samuel 12, author's paraphrase.
3. Swindoll, *Study of James: Practical & Authentic Living,* 17.
4. Philippians 3, author's paraphrase.
5. Ephesians 3, author's paraphrase.
6. Sittser, *A Grace Disguised,* 180.
7. Ibid., 79.

Chapter Eight

1. 2 Kings 4:1–7, author's paraphrase.
2. Chambers, *My Utmost for His Highest,* April 28.
3. Psalm 16, author's paraphrase.

Chapter Nine

1. Hawkins, *Multiple Identities: Understanding and Supporting the Severely Abused,* 1–2.

2. Ibid.

3. Friesen, *Uncovering the Mystery of MPD,* 151–152.

4. Clark, *More Than One,* 37–39.

5. Ibid., 78.

6. Friesen, *Uncovering the Mystery of MPD,* 147.

Chapter Ten

1. Luke 4:14–30, author's paraphrase.

2. Joshua 24, author's paraphrase.

Chapter Eleven

1. Genesis 11–13, author's paraphrase.

2. Chambers, *My Utmost for His Highest,* March 15.

3. Ibid., January 19.

4. Crabb, *Finding God,* p 60.

5. Chambers, *My Utmost for His Highest,* July 6.

BIBLIOGRAPHY

Allender, Dan B. and Tremper Longman III. *Bold Love.* Colorado Springs: Navpress, 1992.

Allender, Dan B. *The Healing Path: How The Hurts In Your Past Can Lead You To A More Abundant Life.* Colorado Springs: Waterbrook Press, 1999.

Beattie, Melody. *The Language of Letting Go: Daily Meditations For Codependents.* New York, HarperCollins, 1990.

Bosch, Henry G. *Our Daily Bread.* Grand Rapids: RBC Ministries, 1995. Reprinted by permission. All rights reserved.

Chambers, Oswald. *My Utmost for His Highest.* Grand Rapids, Dodd, Mead & Co., 1935. Publication rights held by Discovery House Publishers, which is affiliated with Radio Bible Class, Grand Rapids, MI. Copyright renewed 1963.

Clark, Terri A. *More Than One.* Nashville: Oliver-Nelson Books, 1993.

Crabb, Larry. *Finding God.* Grand Rapids: Zondervan, 1993.

Flint, Annie J. (1866-1932), hymn, *He Giveth More Grace*, Orchard Park, NY, in the "Casterline Card" series, number 5510, n.d.

Flora, Steve. "Hearing God's Call." Sermon preached at Garland Alliance Church, Spokane, WA, May 1, 2005.

Friesen, James G. *Uncovering the Mystery of MPD.* San Bernardino: Here's Life Publishers, 1991.

Hawkins, Diane W. *Multiple Identities: Understanding and Supporting the Severely Abused.* Restoration in Christ Ministries. Kearney, NE: Morris Publishing, 2002–2004.

Hoff, B. J. *Thorns & Thrones: Encouraging Words for Faithful Living.* Devotional Calendar, Warner Press, 1991.

Hugo, Victor. *Les Miserables.* Quote by Victor Hugo Penguin Books, New York, NY, 2012. Translated by Norman Denny.

————"A Heart beneath a Stone," Chapter IV in *Les Miserables.* The Literature Network. http://www.online-literature.com/victor_hugo/les_miserables/246/

Lewis, C. S. *The Lion, the Witch and the Wardrobe.* New York, HarperTrophy, 1994.

Long, Brad and Jeanne Kraak. *The Dunamis Course* Student Workbook. Black Mountain, NC, Presbyterian-Reformed Ministries International, 2003.

Lucado, Max. *God Came Near.* Devotional Calendar. Bloomington, MN: Garborg's Publishing, 2000.

Miller, Basil. *Fanny Crosby: Famous Blind Hymn Writer,* in *Ten Girls Who Became Famous.* Grand Rapids: Zondervan, 1946. http://www.truthfulwords.org/biography/crosbytw.html

Peck, Scott. *The Road Less Traveled.* Simon & Schuster, New York, 1980. First published 1978. Http://capone.mtsu.edu/cfrost/god/peck.htm and http://www.goodreads.com/book/show/347852. The_Road_Less_Traveled

Rios, Sandy. "Making Me Strong." *Lord, I Believe.* Cassette Tape, © 1988 Diadem Music.

Roper, David. *Our Daily Bread..* Grand Rapids: RBC Ministries, 2004. Reprinted by permission. All rights reserved.

Sheets, Dutch. *Intercessory Prayer.* Ventura, CA: Regal Books, 1996.

Sittser, Gerald. *A Grace Disguised: How The Soul Grows Through Loss.* Grand Rapids: Zondervan, 1995.

Swindoll, Dr. Charles. *Study of James: Practical & Authentic Living.* Fullerton, CA, Insight for Living, 1991.

Whitson, Stephanie Grace. *Secrets on the Wind.* Bloomington, MN, Bethany House Publishers, 2003.

Willard, Kelly. "Hidden Valleys." *We Believe.* Cassette Tape, © 1991 Sparrow Corporation.

www.ingramcontent.com/pod-product-compliance
Lightning Source LLC
Jackson TN
JSHW080202141224
75386JS00029B/998